GLADYS HOPKINS

DON BRIDDELL

LARRY BARTH

Yellow Shafted Flicker, Arnold Melbye. Photo by Julie O'Neil.

MASTERS OF

Decorative
Bird Carving

MASTERS OF

Decorative
Bird Carving

ANNE SMALL

WINCHESTER PRESS
Tulsa, Oklahoma
1981

For their generous and special contribution of
pen-and-ink sketches for the endpapers, I am very much
obliged to Larry Barth, Don Briddell, Lynn Forehand,
Gladys Hopkins and Arnold Melbye.

Goose feather on colophon page carved by Marc Schultz.
Photo courtesy of the Ward Foundation

Library of Congress Cataloging in Publication Data

Small, Anne, 1928—
Masters of decorative bird carving.

Bibliography: p. 139
Includes index.
1. Wood-carving—United States—History. 2. Decoys
(Hunting)   I. Title
NK9712.S5   745.593   81-16039
ISBN 0-87691-356-7   AACR2

PUBLISHED BY WINCHESTER PRESS
1421 South Sheridan Road
. P. O. Box 1260
Tulsa, Oklahoma 74101

Book design by Quentin Fiore

Printed in the United States of America

1   2   3   4   5   85 84 83 82 81

To Arnold Melbye and the memory of Edith Melbye

Acknowledgments

I acknowledge with deep appreciation the contributions and help of the following individuals and institutions:

Russell Barnard Aitken, New York, New York. Kenneth Basile, Director, North American Wildfowl Art Museum of the Ward Foundation, Salisbury, Maryland. Charles E. Bounds, Salisbury, Maryland. Byron and Maureen Cheever, *North American Decoys*, Spanish Fork, Utah. Elisabeth Clark, Osterville, Massachusetts. Quintina Colio, New York, New York. Connecticut Audubon Society, Fairfield, Connecticut. Mr. and Mrs. Ray Davis, Norwich, Connecticut. Philip de Normandie, Cambridge, Massachusetts. Dr. and Mrs. Daniel Z. Gibson, Chestertown, Maryland. The Wendell Gilley Museum, Southwest Harbor, Maine. Arthur Gould, Chatham, Massachusetts. Dr. J. Lynwood Herrington, Jr., Nashville, Tennessee. Donald B. Howes Antiques, Brewster, Massachusetts. Tom Johnson, Rochester, New York. Morton D. Kramer, M.D., Baltimore, Maryland. John A. Luetkemeyer, Jr., Baltimore, Maryland. Douglas E. Miller, President, Wildlife World, Inc., Monument, Colorado. Maggie Nichols, Associate Managing Editor, *Field & Stream*, New York, New York. Martina R. Norelli, Associate Curator of Prints and Drawings, National Collection of Fine Arts, Smithsonian Institution, Washington, D.C. Mr. and Mrs. Peter Pasky, East Orleans, Massachusetts. Robert M. Peck, The Academy of Natural Sciences of Philadelphia, Philadelphia, Pennsylvania. William Plante, The Plante Company, Warren, Michigan. Dick Sawdo, Woods Hole, Massachusetts. Stephen Tyng, Pleasant Bay Antiques, South Orleans, Massachusetts. The Waterfowl Festival, Easton, Maryland. The Leigh Yawkey Woodson Art Museum, Wausau, Wisconsin.

Preface

Birds predate man by millennia, and therefore represent a tie with all that has come over this planet. The most inspired poets have dedicated their words to the nightingale and skylark. Man, from the Stone Age onward, has depicted the bird on cave walls and coins, in paintings and sculpture. We have worshiped creatures of the sky as being akin to angels. The eagle symbolizes determination and purpose, the dove peace. In its migrations, the bird has been our biannual calendar, a perennial messenger of our change of seasons. On a more basic level, the bird has served us as food, and its feathers have been used for our adornment. To attract birds to fill these mundane needs, North American Indians invented the decoy, about A.D. 1000 constructing out of reeds, feathers, skins, and skeletons—not carving from wood—replicas of waterfowl.

Stemming from these native roots, developing and changing form through succeeding centuries, decoy making reached its zenith in the years between the Civil War and World War I with the carved and painted wooden bird. Among the masters of this craft were A. Elmer Crowell and Lem Ward, who, when protection of migratory waterfowl was legislated between 1913 and 1918 and the need for large rigs of decoys decreased, turned their hands to ornamental and realistic carvings. Other early masters of decorative bird carving such as "Shang" Wheeler, Wendell Gilley, and Arnold Melbye carved decoys for their personal use, but became renowned for their later, ornamental birds.

As we look at the creations in this book we must note the important distinction between decoy making and decorative bird carving: Decoys lure birds; decoratives attract humans. That function dictates form is evident in the differing aspects of the tasks that the carvers set themselves.

Purpose

Decoys were fashioned for the practical purpose of gathering birds for the table or for market, or for sport. Decoratives are intended to demonstrate the union of natural science and artistic skills.

9

Execution

Attitude. The decoy must inspire confidence in its live counterpart. It is shown at ease, with nothing in its pose to alarm its wary target. The viewer of a decorative composition is often pleased by the most dramatic poses, and by confrontations between species.

Coloration. The decoy maker colored his bird to further his ends. The painting pattern was bold and most effective at a distance. For the fowl-in-flight no subtlety was necessary. The creator of the decorative birds shows small details of plumage which invite close scrutiny.

Form. Decoys could be flat, hollow, or half-shapes as if feeding or diving. Feet were rarely represented. Decoratives are three-dimensional, fully contoured, with correct anatomical details, usually including feet.

Conditions. Ice, water, and distance from land influenced the design of decoys. High-breasted decoys were made for the slush ice and strong tides of the Connecticut shore; oversize decoys were set out in the waves ten miles off the Maine coast. These factors do not apply to the decorative's quiet environment of mantel or shelf.

Use. Decoys not only had to be serviceable in the water, but also had to be sturdy and compact enough to withstand rough handling as they were transported to and from the gunning areas in crude carriers or even sacks. On the other hand, an exquisitely long tail or an outstretched wing is a prized detail of a decorative bird.

Size. Decoys were made lifesize or oversize to attract flyers. They were rarely undersize. Decoratives may be any size, though they are rarely oversize.

Subjects. Waterfowl, game birds, and snipe native to the area or appearing during migration were the usual subjects of the decoy maker. The decorative-bird carver reproduces those birds as well as songbirds and the exotics from around the world.

"The Times"

Game laws, environmental considerations, and cultural changes which emphasize preservation and knowledge of our precious natural heritage have combined to turn attention away from the old scenes of market gunning to indoor mantels and shelves. The decorative carver's work reflects these different times and needs.

Art

Birds are not art critics. Therefore the specific intent in the decoy carver's mind was not to create art. That his hands did so is in the eye of the beholder. The maker's mind ordered function; his hands fashioned that which many term Art — naïve as folk art, sophisticated as a Brancusi sculpture. The works shown in this book are neither naïve nor abstract. Their carver's imperative was to fashion and color a sculpture that realistically duplicates the live bird in an artistic way.

Martina Norelli, Associate Curator of Prints and Drawings, National Collection of Fine Arts, Smithsonian Institution, introducing an exhibition of "Art Depicting Birds," states:

> Birds — their power, grace and beauty — have provided an endless source of inspiration for artists. While the bird as subject has evolved beyond a magic symbol and totem, it still possesses a special appeal not often found in relation to other animals.
>
> ... Many of these artists are also ornithologists, some are outdoorsmen, and others sportsmen, and some are museum personnel; all, however, are linked by their inherent interest in birds. Their knowledge of habitat, plumage, anatomy and behavior enables them to produce... carvings that are both artistically satisfying and scientifically accurate. This special capability provides the unique contribution of these accomplished artists.

Though viewed mainly as art, decorative bird carvings open our eyes to the beauty of birds and lead us to an understanding of their value in our lives and the total environment. The bird in the hand lures many to the protection of the bird in the bush. The natural bird's quick movements, manner and flight frustrate the neophyte watcher; the carved bird allows observation at length and at leisure.

The reader will notice that there is scant mention in this book of the prizes won, appearances at exhibits, in print, and on television by the carvers. Suffice it to say that as a group, they have won clusters of honors — so much so that to list their awards would fill a book. Implicit in inclusion in this book is that, by myriad criteria, they are of the top rank.

Though much may be learned by its perusal, this is not a "how-to" book. Bypassing both the workshop and the trophy room, let us proceed to the exhibition hall.

One further note about the carvers: There are important persons in decorative bird carving whose work does not appear in this book. They are the extremely talented carvers of miniatures. These include the late Courtney Allen and A. J. King; also De Gavre, Searles, Sjoholm, and Vreeland, to mention a few. Their creations will be covered in a future volume.

To write about carved birds, one must study birds in their natural habitat when and where possible. Supplementary to this field research is access to the best photography, art, and literature concerning birds and their lives. These observations about the requisites of a writer are brought to mind by the remarkable ornithological scholar who contributed the Foreword to this book.

From the eminent naturalists of the late nineteenth and early twentieth centuries, to to-day's leading ornithologists, from Audubon to acclaimed contemporary bird artists, in no one person are the talents of a writer, artist, teacher, and ornithologist more felicitously combined than Dr. George Miksch Sutton.

One of George Miksch Sutton's first references was Frank M. Chapman's *Bird Life*, and the young naturalist took special notice of Louis Agassiz Fuertes' plates in Florence Merriam Bailey's *Handbook of Birds of the Western United States*.

At age 15 in 1913, Sutton saw his first article in print in *Bird-Lore*, edited by Frank M. Chapman. From 1915 until his untimely death in 1927, Louis Agassiz Fuertes was friend and mentor to Sutton, an association detailed in *To a Young Bird Artist*, published in 1979. Arthur A. Allen, famous for his bird photography, was chairman of the doctoral committee at Cornell University from which George Miksch Sutton obtained his Ph.D. in 1932.

Internationally renowned Professor Emeritus of Zoology at the University of Oklahoma and Curator of Birds at the University's Stovall Museum, Dr. Sutton has written innumerable scientific articles, produced hundreds of drawings and paintings for his own and others' books, and is the author of many books. His latest is *Bird Student*, published in 1980.

For all the honors earned by him, including a knighthood conferred by the government of Iceland in 1972, Dr. Sutton prefers to be described as "a student of birds." He likes "to draw birds and to write." His greatest satisfaction comes, he says, from his work with young people.

It is a boon indeed for this book, its subjects, and its readers that with much grace Dr. George Miksch Sutton consented to write the Foreword. I am deeply grateful to him.

— ANNE SMALL
April, 1981

Foreword

Dr. George Miksch Sutton

My interest in wood carvings of birds goes back to the boyhood day when my Uncle Frank, living at the time on his farm in southern Minnesota, showed me some duck decoys in a neighbor's barn. Most of the decoys were drake mallards, easy to identify by the green head and white ring around the neck, but some were dull and without much pattern, and I suspected that these were hen mallards, but I was bothered by the thought that they might be gadwalls. I knew there was a duck called the gadwall, for I had seen its picture in our big dictionary at home, but I wasn't at all sure how to tell a gadwall from a hen mallard.

Decoys of ducks and geese may well have been what most carvers of birds in America produced in early times, but today a veritable host of men — and a few women — devote themselves to carving, and what they carve are not utilitarian images to be hauled out when opening day arrives, but elegant, highly decorative sculpture notable for its good taste. How the carvers glory in their work! With every stroke of their tools they envision an object that will bring lasting pleasure to those who own it. For every lover of the outdoors a well-carved quail, grouse, or prairie hen will evoke memories of gorgeous days afield in fall or winter. A good pintail carving will remind many a hunter of the morning that started with insipid "bluebird weather," but that turned raw, gray, and exciting when the wind rose sharply, as sprigs and greenwings, tired of being buffeted, came hurtling in overland, wheeled sharply on reaching the pond, and plopped into the water among the reeds as if they no longer intended to go *anywhere*. A killdeer carving will remind every member of the family of the four hard-to-see eggs that someone almost stepped on and of the parent bird's valiant attempts to attract attention away from the nest through feigning injury. More important perhaps than the carvings' ability to stir memories is their power in arguing for protection of that which they represent; for preservation of habitat; for wise laws; for a system of education that will instill in everyone — no matter what his age, profession, or standing as a citizen — a realization that the beauty and wonder and excitement of the world are never to be taken for granted.

The carvings are works of art. Even as fine paintings create an illusion of snow-capped mountains, of lily pads afloat on quiet water, of a dancing girl fussing with the string of her slipper, so do good bird carvings create an illusion of bright-eyed, feather-covered, wondrously alive creatures, some with remarkable shape, some with color patterns lovelier than any man-kind might contrive, some with ornamental crests, whiskers, and spurs fantastic enough to boggle the imagination. This last is hardly an over-statement. That strange South American cotinga known as the umbrellabird is almost a monstrosity. Australia's yellow wattlebird, with its pendant excrescences, makes one wonder what "survival of the fittest" is all about. Even a barnyard rooster, combs, facial flaps, and all, is a whole congeries of improbabilities — yet there he stands, all set to be painted, to be immortalized in a poem, perhaps to be carved! No carver when doing him will stoop to affixing his feathers on a frame. The wood itself is to become the feathers: if hackles, narrow; if tail plumes, broad, thin, and lustrous. The wood itself, properly carved and painted, will create the illusion.

Illusion, yes; not abstraction. I have yet to see a wood carving of a bird that seems to aim at being abstract. The carvers obviously have felt that birds are beautiful, that the special beauty of birds is deserving of close study and analysis, even of out-and-out copying. They have felt no urge to improve on nature, to show that something thought-up can be better than what has actually been seen, to prove that a figure intended to depict swiftness or pomposity or savagery can be more successful as art than a frankly realistic portrait of a peregrine falcon in full stoop, a turkey gobbler puffed up in all his iridescent glory, or a great horned owl glaring at the world while clutching prey.

A good carver insists on accuracy, but he makes no attempt to show every minute detail. At work on a flying goose, he counts the feathers of his model's spread wing; but, knowing that too much fussiness slows action down, he accents not so much the separateness of the quills as the way they all, working together, propel the streamlined body through the air. A good carver knows that the little alula or "bastard wing" at the wrist is important, but that it doesn't always stick up or show even when the bird is flying. He knows that the slotted tips of an eagle's outer primaries curve upward when the great bird is soaring or beating its wings downward, but not at other times. He knows how many bones there are in a bird's toes; that a spotted sandpiper has four toes, a golden plover only three; that in a roadrunner's foot two toes point forward, two backward. He knows that in all herons the hind toe is fairly long and on the same level as that of the three front toes, while in cranes it is small and so far above the level of the front toes that unless the mud is deep only the three front toes leave a track. Details of this sort are important. Not that all bird carvings, even good ones, show them; but every really good carving reveals the fact that its maker has studied and thought hard about his subject, that he has no desire to go beyond realism.

I have, from time to time, found myself wondering how much that passes as nonrealistic art is merely poor drawing or modeling. Some drawing that looks bad may, of course, be inten-tionally so. Picasso's "Bird on Branch" is widely admired as an abstraction, but for me, a student of birds all my life and of art *per se* for about forty years, that painting — which blatantly fails to represent any known species of bird or to let its central figure symbolize freedom, or mastery of the air, or loneliness of life in a cage — also fails as an abstraction since that which is perching on the branch is so unequivocally a bird. The mind that contemplates it is not free. There is no way to dodge or escape from the idea *bird*. No matter how crudely drawn, it is still *bird*. Forced thus to stay within bounds, forced thus to evaluate the bird as such, we can but deplore its ugliness as we sense within ourselves the powerful conviction that Picasso intended that bird to be ugly. What end, we ask, can such a departure from realism serve? Would a beautifully drawn bird, one such as Picasso himself might have drawn during his "academic period," fail as art simply because it aims at capturing a bird's beauty?

Granted that not everything worthy of our respect and attention needs to be beautiful. The bitter, the sweet, rain, and shine are all part of what *is*. Not all great music is melodious. Picasso had every right to draw an ugly bird if he felt that way about his subject matter, but when he drew "Bird on Branch" he was not creating an abstraction. Perhaps, utterly fed up with pretty-pretty drawings of birds, he chose this straightforward way of commenting on the genre.

Turn "Bird on Branch" upside down, with its central figure under rather than above the branch, and for me the picture becomes a stunning abstraction. The central figure is now no longer caricature or caustic comment. Its ruthless stab at pretty drawings of pretty birds is gone. The branch is still there, but what is below the branch no longer forces the viewer to think *bird*. I venture the guess that Picasso liked, really liked, his picture best when it was upside down; that he titled it with tongue in cheek; that he knew full well how controversial it might be.

Now for a story about abstractionism, a true story that may point up some of what I have just said. Soon after moving to this part of the continent about thirty years ago, I had a memorable experience on the University of Oklahoma campus. At a one-man show by John Freed, a young abstractionist painter, I found myself drawn to a certain untitled picture. Why I was attracted I could not say. It was a swirl of whites — grayish white, bluish white, greenish white — nothing more; no central figure of human being, building, or tree half visible through fog; nothing suggestive of foreground, background, sky, or horizon. I told John, whom I'd not met before, that I liked that particular painting. I also told him that I wondered, quite sincerely wondered, why. John looked at me, incredulous at first, then, convinced that I was not teasing, that I truly meant what I had said, he blushed — as if embarrassed, as if confused, as if deeply, somewhat privately pleased. John knew something about me. His professors had told him of my interest in birds. As he went on blushing, by this time almost violently, he said, "Do you know, Dr. Sutton, that painting is the only painting in my show that's of a bird?"

Well... there certainly was nothing in John's picture that looked like a bird. But for me the delicate colors and swirl had been irresistible. Had the stark, unremitting whiteness of it all called to mind blizzards — specifically the last wild blizzard of the winter of 1929–30, a blizzard I could never forget? During that savage storm a flock of 200 snow buntings had returned to their far northern breeding ground, all of them tired, hungry, and eager to find shelter close to the little frame building in which the chief trader, his son, and I were living at the Hudson's Bay Company's Southampton Island trading post. The pretty little things had found something to eat and sand for their gizzards in the snow-free canyon the wind had gouged out below the kitchen window. I had helped to capture the whole flock—all but the few that the husky dogs had gulped. And the flock had lived indoors with us while the gale lasted, singing their hearts out when the sun finally broke through the clouds. Was it *they* that I was seeing as I looked at John's swirl of whites?

John and I became friends. Indeed, I found myself genuinely interested in him and his work. Through him I became convinced that the urge to get away from copying, to free oneself of representationalism, could be sincere.

I have gone into detail on all this because it says something about the *raison d'être* of abstract art. John's swirl of whites was for me a true abstraction. It was not much more of a picture than a stretched canvas without paint would have been. It must have freed my mind completely, letting me *feel* pervasive whiteness, then blizzard, then snowbirds. This is as close as I can come to an explanation.

Carvers of birds in America, realizing that there is no need for them to become abstractionists to prove that they are artists, will go right on creating objects of beauty that look wonderfully like living birds. What they, the creators, are called is of little consequence. It is what they create that is important.

Contents

1

The Old Choppers

"The Old Choppers" one of their number calls them, those earliest masters of decorative bird carving. Yet the art is new enough that of the carvers whose work is shown in this book, all are alive except A. Elmer Crowell (1862–1951), Charles E. "Shang" Wheeler (1872–1949), Ira Hudson (1873–1949), and William Birk (d. 1980).

Both Elmer Crowell of East Harwich, Massachusetts, and Shang Wheeler of Stratford, Connecticut, have been called "the father of decorative bird carving." Whoever might be the true progenitor (the wheel was "invented" more than once, in more than one place) their body of work differed markedly.

Crowell was a market gunner and sportsmen's guide by profession, whose work included making decoys of ducks, geese, and shorebirds. Their success in attracting their own kind was equaled, and later surpassed, by their allure to humankind. As the shooting of migratory waterfowl became more and more restricted by legislation from 1913 on, Crowell found a market for more detailed, ornamental decoys, and for a great variety of birds from herons to hummingbirds. He was so prolific a carver—of lifesize, halfsize, any-size replicas, though miniatures predominate—that it is possible (though costly) to obtain "a Crowell" at auction and antique shops today.

Very few of the artists in this book have had any formal artistic training. Crowell had some twenty lessons one summer in his youth, but aside from that, he is almost entirely self-taught. Crowell's oil paintings of local hunting and boating areas—woodcock rising, quail feeding, fish leaping—are as highly-prized as his carvings, especially as there are many fewer paintings.

Shang Wheeler was a state legislator, manager of an oystering firm, inventor, political cartoonist (his main target: stream pollution), and sportsman. He carved decoys for himself and to give to his friends. Wheeler won the top awards in the decoy contests from the Grand Cham-

A. E. Crowell's lifesize *Great Blue Heron*. Photo by Hugo Poisson.

A. Elmer Crowell, East Harwich, Mass.

"Shang" Wheeler cartooning. Photo courtesy of Connecticut Audubon Society.

Oldsquaw Drake, "Shang" Wheeler. Photo courtesy of Connecticut Audubon Society.

pionship in the first American Decoy Show in Bellport, Long Island in 1923 to the Grand Prize at the National Sportsman Show in 1947. He won a ribbon at the latter show in 1948 with a stunning pair of oldsquaws, after which he decided to retire from competition. (The top award that year went to the Ward brothers.)

Shang produced decoys of almost every species of waterfowl and shorebird hunted in his area, and one sandhill crane exhibited in the Abby Aldrich Rockefeller Folk Art Collection at Williamsburg, Virginia.

A natural artist, Wheeler had only one art lesson, after which he knew he'd gotten the hang of it. Long before he died, his birds were sought by collectors as well as gunners. Shang carved birds intended to be appreciated as art, and he took pride in his achievements.

23

Flying Pintail, Ira Hudson. Photo by Quintina Colio.

Ira Hudson, the most prolific of the Chincoteague, Virginia decoy makers, was noted for the elaborate and fine detail and painting of his carvings of ducks, geese, brant, and yellow-legs. Examples of his flying pintail drakes and a merganser mark Hudson as an early master of decorative bird carving.

Oldtime hunter-carvers knew their subjects—waterfowl and game and shore birds—from countless hours of observation and hands-on contact. The hands that held the carving tools had held the living, or very recently shot, bird. Many of these men were skilled at taxidermy. Gilley and Melbye thought the skins were too pretty to throw away. Well-mounted specimens and well-preserved skins are useful for determining facts such as the correct number of feathers in a wing, but in even the best mounts there is shrinkage and fading which can mislead the un-informed carver. The early masters had no books, no classes, no instruction; they used hand

24

Preening Pintail, Lem Ward. Photo by Jerry Fine.

tools for the most part. Their homework was done in the field and trial-and-error completed their education.

Lem Ward of Crisfield, Maryland, to whom paternity in the art of decorative bird carving is also attributed, is well-known through countless articles in periodicals, television interviews, awards and honors, and two books dealing with the decoys fashioned by Lem and the late Steve Ward. The Ward Foundation and Wildfowl Art Museum in Salisbury, Maryland, was founded in their honor, and in 1974 they were awarded honorary doctorates by Salisbury State College.

It is Lem who is responsible for the decoratives in the larger number of carvings produced by the brothers. He wanted to make a "pretty bird," a "duck to *be* a duck," and he got the notion to carve species other than local waterfowl. Though Lem started to make a few ornamentals on order only as early as the 1920's, the changeover from decoys took place in the 1950's. By 1965 he was making highly decorative carvings of almost every species of North American ducks, the

Yellowlegs, Lem Ward. Photo by Jerry Fine.

Canada goose in many poses, gamebirds, and a few shorebirds, including a yellowlegs and a Hudsonian curlew.

His painting produced "the exact softness of feather effect as in life," he wrote another carver. "With this effect, your birds will breathe; without it they are dead." He carved the entire body — an upraised wing and all — from a single block; only the head, neck, and feet were worked separately. For the sunbathing yellowlegs, Lem carved the bill, head, body and wings from a single block of wood; in Lem's words, "the bill was never released from the wings."

Lem Ward feels that painting is his special gift, a talent which extends to oils on canvas — waterfowling scenes that are owned by a few fortunate friends. Everyone who meets Lem feels that another great gift may be of friendship, his extending his praise, his help to so many fellow carvers and a legion of admirers.

Generosity seems to be in the genes of master carvers. None of those I've met thinks his or her success would be diminished by sharing techniques and information. They have confidence in their individuality. If I make this point in reviewing the earlier masters, it is because they are most often turned to for advice.

Barn Owl, Wendell Gilley. Photo by Dori Selene Rockefeller.

Flying Quail, Wendell Gilley. Photo by Dori Selene Rockefeller.

The Old Choppers

Wendell Gilley of Southwest Harbor, Maine, for many years has shared his knowledge of bird carving with visitors to his workshop and through four editions of his book *Bird Carving: A Guide to a Fascinating Hobby*, first published in 1961. By then Gilley, entirely self-taught, had been carving birds of nearly every North American species in every scale for more than thirty years. He knew birds, and he acquired skill in taxidermy (by correspondence course) and woodworking. After seeing an exhibit of A. E. Crowell's duck carvings in Boston in 1930, Gilley was inspired to start carving in earnest. Continuing his occupation of plumber until the mid-1950's, he made some sales from his home and through Abercrombie & Fitch in New York City.

To date, Wendell Gilley has carved more than 6,000 birds, which have flown to Europe and Canada as well as all over the United States. A number have been presented to heads of state and world leaders.

The bird that comes to mind first when Wendell Gilley's name is mentioned is the bald eagle, but a list of carvings exhibited at The Academy of Natural Sciences of Philadelphia in 1976 — *Downeast Carvings* by Wendell Gilley — includes thirty-eight species. Songbirds, herons, woodcock, owls, ducks, and shorebirds were just a sampling of his enormous output.

Fortunately, a choice group of more than 200 of his birds was kept by Gilley, and they form the nucleus of the collection of The Wendell Gilley Museum opened near his home in Southwest Harbor in 1981. Wendell Gilley says, "I'm a plumber." After April 1981 he can style himself a doctor, for the University of Maine has conferred on him the degree of Doctor of Humane Letters.

Harold Haertel, born in 1904 in Illinois, still lives close to the Fox River where he first observed many species of ducks in his boyhood. He is known for his meticulously accurate working decoys which have never been available commercially, his replicas of the extinct passenger pigeon, as well as mourning doves and decorative ducks and shorebirds. A collection of twenty-one species pairs of ducks in halfsize took Haertel three years to produce. He says, "the shorebirds with legs and feet are as 'fancy' as I prefer to go in decorative birds." His present undertaking is a set of stick-up decoys of all the North American shorebirds for exhibit at Wildlife World in Monument Hills, Colorado. There is a practical use, also, for Haertel's stick-up decoys; they lure their kind in, so that they can be banded.

Arnold Melbye of South Yarmouth, Massachusetts, now 72, began his study of birds as a child when he posed and drew pictures of the gamebirds his father brought home. At that young age, Melbye wanted to record what a wing, say, looked like and how it worked, presaging the precision and accuracy of his carving and painting in later years.

This artist, called by many of his fellow carvers "the dean of versatile bird carving," has brought the sure touch of chisel and paint brush to his earliest carvings of lifesize flying ducks done in the 1930's and 1940's and to the gamebirds, shorebirds, and songbirds which have become his forte.

When asked the three most important rules of decorative bird carving, Arnold Melbye says they are: 1) Study the bird. 2) Study the bird. 3) Study the bird. *Then* come the three aspects

Marbled Godwit, Arnold Melbye. Photo courtesy of Wildlife World, Inc.

of the actual work: carving, painting, posing. He thinks he has done a good job of "removing wood" if the carved bird can be identified before it is painted.

His objective is to create a bird that "an ornithologist can study and be completely satis-fied with," and Melbye is a master of *trompe l'oeil* painting. So successful is he in "fooling the eye" of the observer, that at least one person who knows Melbye's carvings intimately still feels com-pelled to touch a bird to make sure that the feathers aren't incised.

Another hallmark of a Melbye bird is its perfect balance, which the maker considers an essential factor in achieving a lifelike quality from every angle. Usually in tranquil poses, the birds are, however, never static. Such is Arnold Melbye's thorough understanding of his carv-ings' live counterparts.

Evening Grosbeak, Arnold Melbye. Photo by Julie O'Neil.

Mourning Dove, Arnold Melbye. Photo by Julie O'Neil.

2

The Major Shows

In a photograph which appears in *Birds in Our Lives*, published by the U.S. Department of the Interior in 1966, a man and a woman are standing in front of an exhibit of birds carved by Arnold Melbye. The man is holding the brochure for the first show devoted to American decorative bird carving.

This American bird carving exhibit, sponsored by the Kent County chapter of the Maryland Ornithological Society, was held in the Parish House of Emmanuel Protestant Episcopal Church in Chestertown, Maryland, in November 1965. Dr. Daniel Z. Gibson, President of Washington College, Chestertown, and exhibit chairman, and Mrs. Edward Mendinhall, President of the Kent County Chapter of M.O.S., assembled and presented "the most representative exhibition of American bird carvings of this kind ever assembled." They did so in consultation with Wendell Gilley, who, as President of the National Woodcarvers' Association, knew the established carvers of the day—not more than thirty in number.

Lemuel T. Ward, Jr., Gilley, Arnold Melbye, and Harold Haertel displayed their work along with other carvers who have continued to grow in prominence: William Birk, Charles Donald Briddell, Bruce Burk, William E. "Ted" Hanks, Davison B. Hawthorne, Charles Joiner, Jr., Oliver J. "Tuts" Lawson, Paul Nock, William L. Schultz, and John Zachmann.

Not only was the show enthusiastically well-attended, but the carvers themselves were delighted at the chance to meet one another, see one another's work and to talk shop. A widely circulated photograph was taken of Lem Ward, Wendell Gilley and Arnold Melbye. Wendell Gilley wrote, "It is an honor for me to be photographed right between two of the country's finest bird carvers . . . It will be one of the highlights of my life." Lem Ward penned, "I never dreamed that I would meet all the great carvers of our country . . . the snapshot of Melbye, Gilley and myself will be framed and placed where I can tell people who come to my shop, 'Look at this. Here I am in a picture with two of the greatest carvers of our country.'" Arnold Melbye is proud to be pictured with two men he admires so greatly.

The gratifying response to the 1965 show led its founders to sponsor a second exhibit in 1967, at which the original group of carvers was augmented by a dozen or more carvers including

The 1965 Chestertown show. *Left to right:* Lem Ward, Wendell Gilley, and Arnold Melbye.
Photo by Morton D. Kramer, M.D.

Gladys Black, Dan Brown, William I. Tawes, J. Newnam Valliant, Courtney Allen, and General Braddock De Gavre, the last two known for their miniatures.

Attendance more than doubled, and it was clear that it was an idea whose time had come. The facilities at the Parish House were no longer adequate so the third show in 1969 was held at the newly dedicated Daniel Z. Gibson Fine Arts Center at Washington College. The three non-competitive Chestertown shows proved that there was great interest in decorative carved birds. The shows drew people from several states and Canada.

It was evident that the public would support a much expanded show. Stimulated by what they had seen at the Chestertown shows, many more carvers wished to participate, and,

The 1975 exhibition sponsored by the Ward Foundation. Photo by Orlando Wootten, courtesy of the Ward Foundation.

in Salisbury, Maryland, there was a movement to honor Lem and Steve Ward by creating a foundation in their names.

In 1968, the Ward Foundation was established, and in October that year the first Atlantic Flyway Waterfowl and Bird Carving Exhibit was held in Salisbury for the benefit of the foundation and the Wicomico Bird Club.

In conjunction with what became the annual Wildlife Carving and Art Exhibit (later still, the Wildfowl Carving and Art Exhibit), the Ward Foundation in 1971 inaugurated the World Championship Wildfowl Carving Contest. The souvenir program for 1976 proclaimed: "1976 World Championship Contest goes decorative...Officials (of the contest) have noticed for years more and more enthusiasm for decorative carvings over the more traditional decoys... This year saw the strongest swing ever to decoratives."

William J. Mackey, Jr., author of *American Bird Decoys* (E.P. Dutton, 1965), judged many decoy carving competitions. Yet this recognized authority on, and devotee of, decoys, prophesied the trend toward decoratives and strongly encouraged the rule changes that would "allow birds with fragile bills and tails and wings," to quote Harold Haertel. Haertel adds, "I was present in Davenport, Iowa when Bill Mackey first insisted that such changes be made... Without Bill Mackey's influence the present-day carvers, the younger ones, would not be carving today...There were many people and many factors involved, but only one man stands out far above all the others."

The first annual Waterfowl Festival was organized in 1971 at Easton, Maryland, by residents of Talbot County to benefit Ducks Unlimited. The entire community works to present wildfowl and bird carvings and art in the area along the Atlantic Flyway where thousands of ducks, geese, and swans winter.

All the long-established annual decoy shows now include decorative bird categories as well as the traditional decoy classes. Invitational and juried, non-competitive exhibitions attract large and growing numbers of enthusiastic spectators every year.

In 1976 the Birmingham Museum of Art in Alabama mounted an exhibit, "A Native American Art Form, Refined." In the show booklet, Maggie Nichols, Associate Managing Editor of *Field & Stream*, declared, "Though its decoy parentage is evident, this precocious offspring of an old American craft has left the nest and established an existence of its own."

The Leigh Yawkey Woodson Art Museum in Wausau, Wisconsin, established its annual Bird Art Exhibit in 1976. In 1979 the Women's Committee of the Academy of Natural Sciences in Philadelphia instituted the Philadelphia Wildfowl Exposition.

From the 1979 Bird Art Exhibit at the Leigh Yawkey Woodson Art Museum, the works of ten carvers were selected for inclusion in 1980 in the National Fine Arts Collection, Smithsonian Institution, "Exhibition of Art Depicting Birds."

Across the country museums of natural history and of fine arts are acquiring and putting on permanent display, or sponsoring loan exhibitions of, these wonderful sculptures. It is realized that the combination of natural science and artistic skill is a very popular attraction.

36

3

The Decade of the 1960's

Why do you carve birds? What makes you carve birds? How did you get started carving birds? When did you get started? Some carvers are very articulate and specific when answering such questions. Others let their carvings speak for them—whatever they can, or will, reveal about themselves is in their work.

The expressed reasons vary: Lem Ward, beaming, told me, "It's the easiest thing in the world; it's creative!" He cannot mean "easy" in the usual sense of the word. For the truly gifted, perhaps the word is "irresistible." If it is possible to create, it is impossible not to.

Picture Wendell Gilley as a youngster being followed around by the mallard ducklings his father let him adopt. While the ducks were being imprinted by their human "parent," Gilley was being imprinted by them.

For many carvers, decoys made for hunting were the forerunners of later decorative bird carvings.

Not infrequently, the reply to the queries above was, "My wife asked me to carve a bird for her for Christmas. *She* knew I could do it." There was also this response given by a number of carvers: "I saw some carved birds at an exhibit and thought, 'I could do better.'"

Robert Phinney writes on the inspiration for his "Black Scoters": "From the bone chilling, risky drama of scoter-eider hunting, I want to distill for rich, lasting recollection the beauty of their being alive, and to assuage my shame for killing them...Scoter seem so admirably to mock the harshest elements—flying, shifting, and diving for mussels beneath ocean breakers that smoke in bitter February winds. I, too, was surviving on the Bay of Fundy."

COL. C.C. AILES, DEVON, PENNSYLVANIA.

Not surprisingly, the urge to create rather than to destroy can be important to a military man. While in service in three wars, C.C. Ailes took up his childhood hobby of carving.

Sharp-shinned Hawk, C. C. Ailes. Photo by Tom Johnson.

His study of birds began with boyhood trips to the mountains in Pennsylvania with his father. Ailes continued his observations in the almost forty countries in which he was stationed. He is also a trained artist and was a member of the Salmagundi Club in New York City, a professional artists' association.

Ailes' worldwide travels are evident in the wide array of subjects he chooses for his many carvings. They range from the arctic tern—"the loveliest bird in the world," he says—to a turquoise and green Peruvian racket-tail hummingbird.

WILLIAM BIRK (D. 1980), BRIDGEPORT, CONNECTICUT.

Bill Birk grew up on the Susquehanna River near York, Pennsylvania. Early in his life he was a most accomplished woodworker. Naturally he made decoys to hunt with, but he also fashioned violins and other string instruments.

When he went to Connecticut to work for Remington Arms, Birk found himself in another fabled waterfowling area. It was Shang Wheeler country, where interest in decoys was intense on both practical and artistic levels.

Emperor Penguins, C. C. Ailes. Photo courtesy of Roger Tory Peterson.

A miniature mallard carved for his wife got Birk into bird carving in the early 1950's. His first lifesize mallard was sold through Abercrombie & Fitch, and he entered the major decoy contests which were reinstated in the 1960's. Birk, surrounded by "smoothies," pioneered by *carving* the feathers on his birds.

Combining his avocation with his work at Remington, Birk carved all species of waterfowl and game birds. He was an exhibitor at the first show dedicated to decorative bird carving held in Chestertown, Maryland in 1965. In 1975 he showed at the first Bird Carvers Exhibition sponsored by the Connecticut Audubon Society in Fairfield, Connecticut. Birk's wood duck drake became famous worldwide when it was pictured on the 1969 Remington Arms calendar circulated to sportsmen in many countries.

Men predominate in the art of decorative bird carving. This should surprise no one, but its applicability here is that comparatively few women have tramped the fields and marshes in pursuit of game and fowl. Hunters and waterfowlers gain knowledge of all creatures in their

Blue Goose, William Birk. Photo by Anne Small.

White Front Goose, William Birk.

natural surroundings, not just the quarry for their bag. Gladys Black and Kitty Bradshaw are pioneers for their sex in this art.

There are several prominent husband-and-wife teams in which both agree that the woman's part is equal and indispensable. Without *her*, there would be no *him* listed among the masters, and vice versa.

Jan Calvert, of Perryville, Maryland, Carol Ferrin of Pueblo, Colorado, and Eileen Conn of Sedona, Arizona, have established reputations on their own in the past few years, as have a few other women carvers, such as Gladys Hopkins and Lynn Hannon.

Passenger Pigeons, Gladys Black. Photo courtesy of Wildlife World, Inc.

GLADYS BLACK, WARREN, NEW JERSEY.

Gladys Black's childhood in a rural area hunting and fishing with her father and brother gave her the familiarity with waterfowl she later displayed in the carvings she took to the decorative divisions of the U.S. National Decoy Contests. She literally became the First Lady, winning awards with her earliest entries.

Examples of her work range from the hooded mergansers she exhibited at the 1967 Chestertown show, the passenger pigeons shown at the U.S. National Decoy Contest in 1969, to golden crown kinglets at the Ward Foundation's 1974 Wildfowl Carving and Arts Exhibit, and a brown thrasher at a bird carving exhibition sponsored by the Connecticut Audubon Society in 1976. Her ambition to depict all the birds native to New Jersey has been combined with lecturing on wildlife and its art.

The Decade of the 1960's

KITTY BRADSHAW, CRISFIELD, MARYLAND.

Hailing from a waterfowler's "mecca," Kitty Bradshaw knows her ducks and geese. Studying art privately and at the Art Student's League in New York City, she became a portrait painter first, then a carver. Her art has won numerous awards and tributes. A favorite compliment to her art came from a live pintail which attacked, as a rival, a pintail carved by Bradshaw. In her spare time, she emulates her models by taking to the water and the air. She is an expert swimmer and a licensed pilot of her own small plane.

Sunning Pintails, Kitty Bradshaw.

Garud Chetti, Sparrow Hawk, Don Briddell.

DON BRIDDELL, MT. AIRY, MARYLAND.

Charles Donald Briddell, listed in the company of those who exhibited in the first Chestertown show in 1965, is prominent in the world of bird carving. He grew up in Crisfield, Maryland, with free and informal access to Lem and Steve Ward to whom, he believes, all today's carvers of decorative birds are in debt. It is typical of the Wards that they were not satisfied with Don's work until he showed his own "mark."

Briddell expresses his feelings about his work:

At one time I treated Nature in a mindless and abusive way. Even so, it never refused me . . . . Though I no longer hunt . . . it is interesting to me that the function of a decoy is to bring Nature (ducks) into the grasp of men. The evolution [of the decoy into today's highly articulated decorative carving] has reversed the role of this block of wood. Now its purpose is to bring men back . . . to Nature . . . Unlike a stuffed bird that reeks of death, a carving can be full of life.

The work is not to be understood as an end in itself. It only points to that which is real.

44

American Bittern, Dan Brown.

Yellowlegs, Dan Brown.

DAN BROWN, SALISBURY, MARYLAND.

With his long-time customers and new admirers crowded around his table at a prestigious wildfowl art exhibition, Dan Brown smiles and resumes writing a sketch of a fellow carver to meet a journalist's deadline.

Self-taught, a longtime duck hunter and decoy maker, Brown started exhibiting at major shows and winning awards in 1966. More and more detail in his carving and painting put Brown into the decorative categories and his ornamental waterfowl have been joined by shorebirds and songbirds.

Brown, an alumnus of the second and third Chestertown shows, has lent his name and effort to the success of the Ward Foundation Wildfowl Carving and Art Exhibit from the first show in 1948 and is a regular participant in the Waterfowl Festival at Easton, Maryland.

In contributing the first-hand account of the activities of his friend, Delbert "Cigar" Daisey, for the decorative waterfowl section of this book, Dan Brown provides an authentic picture of a natural artist in every sense.

46

BRUCE BURK, GRASS VALLEY, CALIFORNIA.

Failing to find a duck carving suitable for a lamp for his den, Bruce Burk undertook his first carving. Burk wanted a mallard shown with wings and feet outstretched for a landing. He began his task with the zest of a novice, and the precision and skills of the engineer he was.

He also brought to the task knowledge of waterfowl gained as a boy in North Dakota, which he honed by painting pictures of the creatures for several years and by studying endless photographs.

By the mid-1960's Burk had sold several hundred of his carvings on both coasts and was invited to exhibit in the Chestertown shows. Noticing the intense interest these and succeeding exhibits aroused in would-be carvers and collectors, Burk made an invaluable contribution to the art. He wrote *Game Bird Carving*, dedicated to Lem and Steve Ward, Wendell Gilley, and Arnold Melbye, published in 1972. Through many editions it has become a standard in the field. In 1976 Winchester Press brought out Burk's *Waterfowl Studies*, another important resource for waterfowl artists among others. His hobby having become his vocation, Bruce Burk has interrupted his carving and painting to revise *Game Bird Carving* to include new techniques and tools developed in the past decade.

Wood Duck Pair, Bruce Burk. Photo by Bruce Burk.

Gyrfalcon, Thomas Carlock, presented to the Air Force
Academy. Photo by Dorn, Inc.

THOMAS CARLOCK, FAIRHAVEN, NEW JERSEY.

In the late 1930's, Thomas Carlock carved some forty working decoys for himself, but did not take up his tools again until 1966 when he entered the decorative bird carving field.

His specialty is birds of prey which he fashions with knife and chisel from one piece of wood, except for legs and feet. Unlike other carvers, who use oils and acrylics, Carlock attains his effects with tempera paints.

Among Carlock's many achievements are his gyrfalcon presented to the Air Force Academy in Colorado for permanent display and his duplication of an eagle from solid Honduran mahogany for the U.S. Senate caucus room.

48

Canada Goose, Thomas Carlock.

THE REVEREND JACK DRAKE, CARLSBAD, NEW MEXICO.

Although his ministry in the Church of God comes first, Drake has been inspired to carve more than 500 birds since he took up the art in the early 1950's.

With no art training — "just got to thinking I could carve a bird" — he developed his talent to the point that his passenger pigeons, a robin, and a lark were on exhibit at the Smithsonian Institution in 1971. In 1976, at a White House dinner held in the Rose Garden, each of the nineteen tables had for a centerpiece a bird carving by Jack Drake.

As part of his lifetime achievement, Drake wants to portray the state bird and flower for all fifty states. With great fidelity to their natural prototypes, his flower petals are translucent. His quail — as all his creations — are so lifelike that a hunting dog once retrieved a Drake-carved quail.

Cardinal Family, Jack Drake. Photo courtesy of Baker Collector Gallery, Lubbock, Texas.

Goshawk with Ruffed Grouse, Jim Foote. Photo courtesy of Wildlife World, Inc.

James E. Foote, Gibraltar, Michigan.

    Jim Foote has been in the right place doing the right thing at the right time. His occupation before he turned to wildlife art as a painter and carver was game biologist for the Michigan Department of Natural Resources. The place was Pointe Mouille where Foote banded thousands upon thousands of migrating ducks. Just at the time when wildlife art was coming into its own, he was prepared. He had the background and the talent to forge a new career — in the art that combines natural science and artistic skill.

    Foote's illustrations and paintings have appeared in many natural resource and wildlife publications. As valued as his carvings, his paintings hang in government and private buildings in Michigan and Washington, D.C.

M.A. Glassford, Scarborough, Ontario, Canada.

    Al Glassford *had* to start carving. He and a fellow gunner shot up the friend's father's decoys accidentally; in a hurry they decided to produce a new rig.

    Once he began carving — and winning prizes — Glassford was hooked, and in 1976 he left high-powered corporate life to make his living in decorative bird carving. He is very knowledge-

Mallard, Ted Hanks.

able about wildlife, very skilled at painting, and very imaginative. One of his earlier creations was "Widgeon Stealing Celery From a Canvasback." His output since includes gamebirds, eagles, owls, and songbirds. A very delicately poised piece is his woodcock attached to a vine by a toe only.

Glassford's carvings appear in the major shows in Canada and the United States. His "Female Hummingbird Feeding Nestlings" was selected from the Leigh Yawkey Woodson Art Museum's 1979 Bird Art Exhibit to be shown in the National Collection of Fine Arts at the Smithsonian Institution's Exhibition of Art Depicting Birds in 1980.

WILLIAM E. HANKS, JEFFERSON, MAINE.

Ted Hanks hails from Oxford, Maryland, where he came by his talent for carving waterfowl naturally. His grandfather, "Ed" Parsons, a ship's chandler and decoy carver, in his later years fashioned beguiling miniature decorative ducks and geese.

Hanks sailed the Chesapeake Bay waters, then joined the navy and took up carving to while away the time. He is retired from the navy, living in Maine, and is devoting his full time (that is, what he can spare from sailing) to carving. He is famous for his flying Canada geese in the Tidewater Inn in Easton, Maryland.

Preening Scaup, Davison Hawthorne. Photo courtesy of Wildlife World, Inc.

53

DAVISON B. HAWTHORNE, SALISBURY, MARYLAND.

A well-known carving by Dave Hawthorne is his fullsize preening scaup which won a first in decoratives at the 1967 International in Davenport, Iowa. His bond with waterfowl was formed as a young boy when he hunted along the south shore of Long Island from a homemade boat thatched with grass.

Hawthorne's acquaintance with birds includes gamebirds, songbirds, and especially shorebirds. Of the latter, his favorite is the lesser yellowlegs. A longtimer in the field, Hawthorne exhibited in the Chestertown shows and can be seen at the North American Wildfowl Art Museum of the Ward Foundation. He is the carver in the film introducing the visitor to the art of wildfowl carving.

Killdeer, Davison Hawthorne. Photo courtesy of Wildlife World, Inc.

Black Neck Stilt, J. J. Iski.

Oldsquaws, J. J. Iski. Photo courtesy of Wildlife World, Inc.

JULIUS J. ISKI, BORDENTOWN, NEW JERSEY.

Perhaps Jules Iski had never heard of the basic precepts of bird carving. This part-time amateur painter admired some prize-winning decoys, thought he'd have a go at it, looked at some pictures and a mount or two, then carved a pair of buffleheads which took First Place in the decorative lifesize class at Babylon, New York, in 1969. It was no fluke as his succeeding work proved; in 1971 his oldsquaws won Best in World at the Ward Foundation competition.

Iski, in spite of his seemingly casual approach, is a perfectionist who started carving when the shift from "smoothies"—painted feathers and wings—to the carving of feathers, body, and tail with raised wings had taken place.

He points out that while *all* poses of a live bird are *natural*, some are awkward. Iski strives to capture the graceful, calm aspect of the waterfowl and shorebirds he carves.

56

The Decade of the 1960's

ROBERT KERR, SMITHS FALLS, ONTARIO, CANADA.

In the early 1950's, Bob Kerr carved decoys for his own use, avid hunter and outdoorsman that he is. By the late 1950's other sportsmen prevailed upon him to sell some of them. As he worked to satisfy his customers, his very detailed ducks became too handsome to be jeopardized in the marshes, and the carvings were displayed indoors.

Throughout the next decade, Kerr found competition much to his liking, for in the top decoy contests in Canada and the United States he won numerous awards. He finally had to give up competing so that he could fill the orders piling up for his birds from individuals and museums.

An early bird, a green-winged teal with its bill buried in its feathers, shows what they were after. Kerr has broadened the scope of his subjects to extend to gamebirds, shorebirds and songbirds.

There were three Canadians among the ten carvers whose work was selected for the Exhibition of Art Depicting Birds at the Smithsonian Institution in 1980. Kerr's blue heron was one of the decorative bird carvings on display at this show sponsored by the National Collection of Fine Arts.

NeNe Goose, Robert Kerr.

Yellow-shafted Flicker, Oliver Lawson.

Oliver J. Lawson, Crisfield, Maryland.

"Tuts" Lawson has been making his living carving birds since he was seventeen. Although his style is his own, he benefited from close association with Lem and Steve Ward. He acknowledges their importance in his career, including Lem's submitting his name for the first Chestertown show in 1965.

Lawson's work now encompasses gamebirds and songbirds as well as waterfowl. His recent creations are intricate compositions of birds and other natural elements—flowers, butterflies—all carved from wood.

At the 1979 Waterfowl Festival in Easton, Maryland, Lawson's "Canada Goose in a Cornfield" displayed in the lobby of The Tidewater Inn, delighted and surprised the spectators. It was hard to believe that the cobs, kernels and husks were carved from wood and not supplied daily from a nearby cornfield.

The Decade of the 1960's

PAUL F. NOCK, SALISBURY, MARYLAND.

Paul Nock, a pioneer in decorative bird carving, was a participant in the first Chestertown show and a co-founder of the Ward Foundation's annual Wildfowl Art Exhibits. His birds were widely displayed and are in demand by collectors, museums, and galleries.

Spurred on by Lem Ward, Nock began carving waterfowl in 1956, and since then has produced countless ducks, geese, gamebirds, shorebirds, and songbirds. He has demonstrated and lectured in the art of bird carving at the Smithsonian Institution and on several television shows.

Nock's interest in photography has been an aid and stimulus to his carving which has brought this genial man many friends and admirers. A most cherished honor was being presented to H.R.H. Princess Anne of Great Britain at her request when she acquired one of his birds.

Least Sandpiper, Paul Nock.

Chickadee, Paul Nock.

ROBERT PHINNEY, BRIDGETOWN, NOVA SCOTIA, CANADA.

Robert Phinney was born in New Jersey and lived for many years in Maine. In 1961 the Kennedy Galleries in New York City mounted a one-man show of his work. He was not yet twenty and had been carving professionally for four years. Much of what follows is extracted from a notebook which Phinney has put together to accompany his birds in the few exhibits in which he participates.

Carving has always been as natural a response to being alive as eating and breathing. At age six, the most personal present for a beloved and convalescent first-grade teacher was a shoebox full of intricately carved and painted insects.

At age twelve I carved the first bird, a swimming goldeneye. Watching and stalking these beautiful ducks all that winter of 1954 demanded the employ of a carved decoy. In spring a carved crow was needed for Grandma's garden.

At age 14, only the most beautiful Canada goose I could carve would express the stupefying infatuation felt for my first girlfriend. The goose was great and so was the disappointment. Somehow she missed the message.

But when Phinney displayed an "assembly line version" of the goose, the replicas sold. He'd had no formal art training, but his Maine neighbor, the American sculptor William Zorach, pointed out the difference between wood carving and sculpting from life. Thus guided and encouraged, Phinney worked with intense dedication.

Before and after the show at the Kennedy Galleries, Phinney had a ready market for his carvings of ducks, sea and shore birds, game, and songbirds.

60

But after two very productive years of carving, in 1963 other matters demanded his attention (education, marriage, the Peace Corps), and not until 1972 with his move to Bridgetown did Phinney find the peace and isolation to resume carving. Only a few collectors own his birds carved from wood, for most of his work in the past decade has been for casting in bronze.

J. RANDOLPH ROWE (1922–1978), WEST LAWN, PENNSYLVANIA.

Randy Rowe was a highly skilled and versatile craftsman. He succeeded at the following occupations: cabinet maker, carver of ornamental gun stocks, and restorer of antiques including musical instruments and clocks. As a hobby he became a pistol and rifle marksman.

When Rowe's physical handicaps were complicated by arthritis and surgery, he was confined to a wheelchair. At that time he turned to professional illustration and carving fulltime. Rowe's accomplishments in these fields were of the first order; his paintings appeared on the covers of *Pennsylvania Game News*, and in 1969 he first exhibited his bird carvings at the third Chestertown show and at the second annual show in Salisbury, Maryland.

His fellow carvers and the public gave his ruffed grouse, done from one piece of wood, the highest praise. Other well-known sculptures of Rowe's are the bald eagle which is the official emblem of the National Rifle Association, a grouping of quail with chicks, and a yellow-shafted flicker with outstretched wings. Many called this talented man, "friend"; at least one friend, Lem Ward, called him, "genius."

Quail, Randolph Rowe. Photo courtesy of Wildlife World, Inc.

61

Green-winged Teal Hen, Ron Rue.

RONALD L. RUE, CAMBRIDGE, MARYLAND.

Ron Rue has carved at least 600 working decoys since 1964, and in addition, he reckons he has carved more than 100 decoratives, waterfowl mostly, at least two dozen songbirds, many miniatures, and 3,225 hunting silhouettes.

Rue, like so many carvers on the Eastern Shore, feels he owes much to his longtime close friendship with Lem and Steve Ward, though he decided early to take heed of their admonition not to "copy their mistakes," as they modestly put it.

Ron Rue's way of carving has won him awards and honors in major shows including eleven of the Ward Foundation's and all ten of the Waterfowl Festivals in Easton. He especially likes the challenge of reproducing the subtle plumage of the females of waterfowl species.

A Baltimore oriole which had flown against a window was brought to Ron. It's Maryland's state bird and he thought it was so pretty that he carved its likeness. At a reception in Queen Anne County, Maryland, for Princess Anne of Great Britain in 1976, the carving was presented to her. Rue was pleased that the English visitor knew the species and was very interested in the American art of decorative bird carving.

Gadwall Hen, Ron Rue.

WILLIAM L. SCHULTZ, SCANDINAVIA, WISCONSIN.

Bill Schultz has an historical overview of decorative bird carving dating from 1948 when he won his first blue ribbon. It was a special triumph because at that time a realistically-carved, naturalistically-posed bird might be rejected as "too fancy."

From 1948 to 1973, Schultz, a member of the staff of the Milwaukee Public Museum, studied birds in their natural habitats throughout the world. He collected and prepared bird specimens, painted backgrounds for the museum's major natural history dioramas, and designed natural history exhibits.

During those years, Schultz also became a top-ranking decorative-bird carver, winning numerous awards and countless blue ribbons.

Kenneth Basile, Director of the North American Wildfowl Art Museum of the Ward Foundation, writes of the "musical quality" of Schultz's work. Let your eye move over the elements of "Bittern with Marsh Wren" and feel its rhythm. Trace the circularity of "Limpkin with Gallinule."

Since 1973, Schultz has devoted himself to carving fulltime for Wildlife World in Colorado.

63

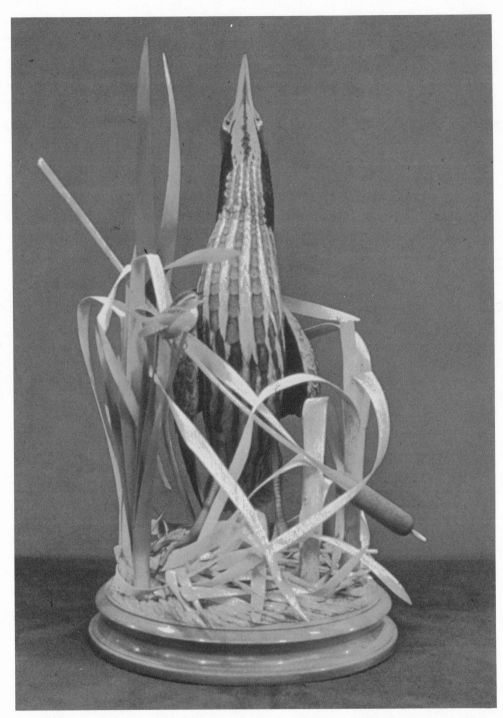

Bittern with Marsh Wren, William L. Schultz. Photo courtesy of the Ward Foundation.

Bald Eagle, Wendell Gilley. Photo by Byron Cheever.

Red-breasted Nuthatches, Arnold Melbye. Photo by Paul Godfrey.

Hummingbird, A. E. Crowell. Photo by Theodore Small.

Flying Merganser, Ira Hudson. Photo by Quintina Colio.

Classic Preening Yellowlegs, A. Elmer Crowell. Photo courtesy of Pleasant Bay Antiques.

Gold Finches, by Arnold Melbye. Photo by Julie O'Neil.

Peregrine Falcon with Quail, 1969, Lem Ward. Photo by Jerry Fine.

Baltimore Oriole, Arnold Melbye. Photo by Julie O'Neil.

Woodcock, Arnold Melbye.

Prairie Chickens, Bruce Burk.

Justice — Peregrine and Blue Jay, Don Bridell.

Male Pintail, Ronald Rue.

Gray Jays, M. A. Glassford.

Canada Goose in a Cornfield, Oliver Lawson. Photo by Tom Johnson.

Woodcock, M. A. Glassford. Photo courtesy of Wildlife World, Inc.

Scissor-tailed Flycatcher, Jack Drake. Photo courtesy of Baker Collector Gallery.

Cardinals with Magnolia, Oliver Lawson.

Hummingbird, Robert Kerr. Photo by Russell Fink.

Wilson's Snipe, Robert Phinney.

Red-winged Blackbird, Robert Phinney.

Mockingbirds, Jack Drake. Photo courtesy of Baker Collector Gallery.

Limpkin with Gallinule, William L. Schultz. Photo courtesy of Wildlife World, Inc.

Red-breasted Nuthatch, Jack Drake. Photo courtesy of Baker Collector Gallery.

Black-shouldered Kite, William L. Schultz. Photo courtesy of Wildlife World, Inc.

Carolina Parakeets, William L. Schultz. Photo courtesy of Wildlife World, Inc.

Yellow-billed Cuckoo, Eldridge Arnold.

Northern Oriole, Jack Gilmore. Photo by
Walt Anderson.

Clapper Rail, Jack Franco. Photo by
Russell Barnard Aitken.

Nature's Harmony, Pat Godin. Photo by Jim Little.

Great Horned Owls, Larry Barth. Photo by
Tom Johnson.

Ross' Gulls Feeding, E. Lynn Forehand.

Red Jungle Fowl, Lynn Forehand. Photo by Steve Budman, Ward
Foundation. 1979 Best in World, Decorative Lifesize.

Brant, E. Lynn Forehand. Photo by William Plante,
courtesy of Wildlife World, Inc.

4
The Decade of the 1970's

By the 1950's, sportsmen and collectors were willing to pay the prices demanded for decorative birds. Bird and art lovers became an increasingly larger part of the market during the 1960's, followed by investors, and by the 1970's, many people were standing in line for months, even years, to acquire a decorative bird carving from a master.

Where there is demand, there is supply. As many more practitioners entered the field and were able to share ideas through shows and competitions, new techniques and tools were developed. House paints gave way to artists' oils and acrylics; power tools to carve and sand bodies, burning pens to delineate feathers and markings were widely, but not exclusively, adopted.

The concept of action and habitat settings created new challenges: how to suspend several birds in flight; how, and of what substance, to "construct" water of sea or pond to depict diving birds.

As the sky is the limit for the artist's winged subjects, so it is for his imagination.

ELDRIDGE ARNOLD, GREENWICH, CONNECTICUT.

"El" Arnold's career in graphic design distracted him from his true calling—carving birds. These two pursuits require many of the same abilities, including, of course, a very observant eye. An ardent hunter, Arnold stored up impressions of winged creatures until such time as he could release them through sculpture.

He got some pointers from his waterfowling companion, the carver Ken Gleason, then applied himself with great diligence. The first birds Arnold considered presentable were met with much admiration in the shows in which they were entered.

Competition spurs him on, but the essential reason Arnold carves is to capture something of the elusive miracles of nature.

Common Tern, Eldridge Arnold. Photo by Eldridge Arnold.

Woodcock, Eldridge Arnold. Photo by Eldridge Arnold.

Mother Owl, Larry Barth. Photo by Tom Johnson.

LARRY BARTH, RECTOR, PENNSYLVANIA.

Larry Barth's "Great Horned Owls" was a how-to project for his senior year thesis at Carnegie-Mellon University's College of Fine Arts. Barth designed, executed and documented every step of the process from preliminary drawings to final display.

The sequence of slides is marvelously revealing. Barth uses single blocks of wood (for the mother owl four pieces are glued together to make one unit) and carves with chisels and rasps only. He normally doesn't insert feathers but he made an extraordinary exception for the baby owls. He boiled, then *chewed* balsa strips to make their fluffy covering.

Although Barth has carved birds since he was a youngster, he was headed for a career as an illustrator; drawings he did as a teenager appear in a college ornithology textbook. Demand for his carvings, however, led to his determination to create in the three-dimensional form.

76

Baby Owls, Larry Barth. Photo by Tom Johnson.

Ruffed Grouse, Larry Barth. Photo courtesy of Leigh Yawkey Woodson Art Museum.

78

Stretching Sparrow Hawk, Paul Burdette.

PAUL BURDETTE, ORTON, ONTARIO, CANADA.

Paul Burdette, long a city dweller, has made it to the country where he has a wildlife refuge and wildlife art gallery on his sixty-five acre farm.

He started carving as a Boy Scout, later making decoys to use when he could escape the city to go duck hunting. Burdette's entries in decoy contests in Canada and the United States have brought him many prizes, and he credits competition with bringing out his finest skills.

His respect for and realistic awareness of the natural world inspires him to use his talent to reproduce many of its creatures.

"Stretching Sparrow Hawk" was selected to be exhibited at the National Collection of Fine Arts of the Smithsonian Institution in Washington, D.C. in 1980.

Battling Coot, E. Lynn Forehand. Photo courtesy
of Wildlife World, Inc.

E. LYNN FOREHAND, CHESAPEAKE, VIRGINIA.

Lynn Forehand says he is triple-faceted—part artist, part engineer, part ornithologist-naturalist. His ingenious compositions bear this out. His sculptures attest to his artistry: the high tension of "Red Jungle Fowl," the drama of the daily business of life in "Ross' Gulls Feeding," the domestic tranquillity of "Brant."

Forehand could not have carried out his artistic concepts without engineering skills. Look at the balance and structure of "Ross' Gulls Feeding." A steel rod connects the wings of the lower two birds, and the contested-for fish in the bills of the upper birds supports the top bird.

Forehand, the ornithologist-naturalist, tracked down a skin collected on Mindanao in the Philippines in 1887 in order to depict the jungle fowl accurately. His placement of the homely dandelion in such a piece brings us down to earth. (The dandelion fluff is made from dental floss.) Now look closely at the wing-tips of the brant (in color section): those are flies.

Male Bufflehead Diving, Paul Burdette.

81

Mourning Doves, E. Lynn Forehand. Photo by James L. D. Tatum and Associates.

Wren, Jack Franco.

JACK FRANCO, ASSONET, MASSACHUSETTS.

Jack Franco carves many species of birds and waterfowl, but he feels a special kinship with shorebirds, from hours spent on the beach surf fishing. His first carvings were stick-up decoys of these birds. Carving was an enjoyable hobby while he made his living as an art teacher and lobsterman.

When Franco visited the Ward Foundation's World Championship Carving Contest in the spring of 1972, he saw decorative bird carving for the first time, and knew where his future lay. He sought help from experienced carvers. For instance, John Scheeler suggested using fiberglass foam insulation to re-create cattails for one of Franco's compositions.

Russell B. Aitken, a collector of the highly realistic shorebirds Franco now fashions, took the birds down to the marshes and photographed them in their native habitat.

House Finch, Jack Gilmore. Photo by Walt Anderson.

American Kestrel, Jack Gilmore. Photo by Walt Anderson.

JACK C. GILMORE, CARMEL, CALIFORNIA.

Jack Gilmore first modeled scale replicas of the submarines he designed for thirty years. When he retired from naval architecture, he set to carving replicas-in-wood of the birds he attracted to his backyard feeders in Virginia. His first bird, a nuthatch, had no feet, for Gilmore hadn't learned how to make them.

Nearly a decade later, and a continent away, Gilmore has mastered all the details of a bird's anatomy. He carves beaks and bills, as well as feet, from wood, and he uses no power or burning tools.

From his childhood days in Florida, Gilmore has always had a singular rapport with all types of birds so that he has become a versatile carver. His sculptures of waterfowl, owls, quail, pheasants, birds of prey, and many songbirds are joined by their live counterparts such as the tufted titmouse which feeds from Gilmore's hand. When Gilmore sits outside carving, a curious and friendly scrub jay perches on his shoulder.

Black Duck Pair, Pat Godin. Photo courtesy of the Ward Foundation.

PATRICK R. GODIN, BRANTFORD, ONTARIO, CANADA.

Pat Godin is intensely dedicated to his carving on the scientific as well as the artistic level. The idea for his black duck pair came from the ecological research he did for his master of science degree. He learned that the hen's need for protein far exceeds the male's; hence she is feeding on a dragonfly nymph while the drake remains alert and watchful for predators. The positional arrangement reflects the fact that the female of a mated pair usually leads the male on water as in flight.

To extend the limits of his imagination and knowledge of nature, Godin has made the transition to lifesize, realistic bird sculpture. "Nature's Harmony" puts the viewer on scene in the delicate ecosystem of the cattail marshes of the prairie pothole regions of central Canada and the United States. Among the area's habitual nesting inhabitants are the American widgeon and the yellow-headed blackbird.

86

The Decade of the 1970's

WILLIAM HANEMANN, METAIRIE, LOUISIANA.

Examine "Day's End" (color section) and you will find out more about the carver than words can tell. He is acquainted with the school of *trompe l'oeil* painting, he enjoys historical research, he reveres the traditions of his native soil, and he is endlessly painstaking. Everything— the leather bag, the rusty nail, the enamel mug, the ceramic jug, the limp ducks — is carved from wood.

Hanemann takes particular care in selecting the wood for all his carvings. In this case he used ten different species including Tupelo gum, cypress, Honduran mahogany, Spanish cedar, basswood, birch, fir, and a South American wood.

Hanemann feels that something of the artist's individuality is an essential component of a sculpture.

Yellow-billed Cuckoo, Lynn Hannon. Photo by Jim Angel.

Territorial Dispute, Lynn Hannon. Photo by Jim Angel.

LYNN HANNON, ODESSA, FLORIDA.

Lynn Hannon is articulate about the art form of decorative bird carving and about her work in it:

> We have such a unique opportunity in this art form. It is so new that everything seems to be innovative. Every move seems to be a giant step.
>
> There is nothing that serves as well as close observation of live birds to give the artist a perception of the subtle composition that suggests "life" . . . a deep understanding of the aerodynamics, and the flex and working of wings and feathers.
>
> The fantastic ability of the yellow-billed cuckoo to dart through the most dense thicket is expressed by the dagger-like thorns on the vines through which he flies.
>
> There is no one way to work. The artist must be the servant of necessity, no matter how hard the master.

Indeed. To complete just one wing of the red-shouldered hawk took Hannon 1,200 hours; the entire composition some 4,000 hours.

The Decade of the 1970's

MARK HOLLAND.

When Mark Holland lived on Cape Cod, Massachusetts, he maintained an aviary for waterfowl and spent hours in his canoe, floating silently at the whim of tide and water, observing shorebirds in their natural surroundings.

No permanent address is given for Mark; he has taken his canoe to the West Coast and Texas to study and carve western birds. The following is his description of his first sight of whooping crane from his craft:

> They were quite watchful for about five minutes, so I waited them out. I was able to finally beach the canoe right in front of them, less than 60 feet away! At one point one just stared at me as I sat in the canoe. I wondered how many humans had ever been that close to this magnificent bird...there are about two hundred in the world. I would love to.carve a lifesize one with wings extended in courtship dance.

Ring Neck Plover, Mark Holland. Photo by T. Small.

89

Yellow-throated Warblers, Jack and Bette Holt. Photo by Tom Johnson.

Spotted Sandpiper Catching Crane Fly, Jack and Bette Holt. Photo by Tom Johnson.

JACK AND BETTE HOLT, WILMINGTON, DELAWARE.

Jack and Bette Holt attended the first Chestertown show in 1965 as eager-to-learn visitors. They met and talked with Wendell Gilley, Lem Ward, Arnold Melbye, and the other experienced carvers. Attending every show and demonstration available, the Holts soaked up information like pine absorbs paint, and this team was on its way, Jack carving, Bette painting.

The Holts' years of bird watching with eye and camera enable them to pose their creations simply and realistically. Though they carve birds of many species and families, songbirds are their specialty.

For the past decade, Jack and Bette Holt have been on the exhibitor's side of the table at the major annual shows at Salisbury and Easton, Maryland. They have also participated in special exhibits at the Kodak Gallery in New York City, at the Birmingham Museum of Art in Birmingham, Alabama and at the Philadelphia Wildfowl Exposition.

White-breasted Nuthatch, Gladys Hopkins. Photo by
Dale James.

GLADYS HOPKINS, NATICK, MASSACHUSETTS.

Gladys Hopkins cannot bandsaw the basic shape of a bird out of a block of basswood until she knows what it eats, whether its feathers are truly red, or only appear to be because they reflect light, or scatter light as iridescent feathers do. There is no such thing as an insignificant detail of a bird's behavior and environment. She considers every facet to be enormously important to a lifelike rendering of her subject.

Reversing the usual order, Hopkins cast birds when she started out. With her exhaustive research and exquisite attention to detail, she was not producing enough to keep a chickadee alive, so she taught herself the casting process and made small limited editions of ducks, gamebirds, shorebirds, and songbirds.

With an established reputation, Hopkins has resumed carving one-of-a-kind sculptures. Among her subjects are a red-breasted nuthatch, red poll, singing song sparrow and a pair of cedar waxwings. Perhaps a house finch, too. She wrote a friend, "I have this cat-captured house finch living in the bathroom, and it likes to remove all the seeds from the tin and drop them on the floor, one by one...plink...plink..."

92

The Decade of the 1970's

William J. Koelpin, Hartland, Wisconsin.

William Koelpin, self-described as an "ardent sportsman," is zealous in the pursuit of all knowledge that will ensure accuracy in his artistic representations of gamebirds. Consider his carvings as they bear out the words of Neltje Blanchan, a nineteenth-century naturalist whose books are still most readable. In *Game Birds* Blanchan writes of the Canada spruce grouse that "they give themselves grand airs, tail quills rustling like silk, drooped wings . . . a miniature impersonation of self conceit."

On prairie chickens:

> Westward the prairie chicken . . . takes its way . . . Early in the morning in the spring the booming of males assembled on the "scratching ground" — some slight elevation of the prairie — summons the hens from that territory to witness their extraordinary performances until the whole region re-echoes with the sound [that is] like deep tones from a church organ . . . After a week of circus and concert the cocks usually fall to fighting . . . scattering feathers as they leap into the air.

Eastward, Koelpin's "Greater Prairie Chickens" took their way to the National Collection of Fine Arts in the Smithsonian Institution for the Exhibition of Art Depicting Birds in 1980.

Pied-bill Grebe with Young, William J. Koelpin. Photo by Hans Keerl Studio.

Greater Prairie Chickens, William J. Koelpin. Photo by Hans Keerl Studio.

Canadian Spruce Grouse, William J. Koelpin.

Hanging Mallard, Roy Le Gaux.

ROY LE GAUX, SLIDELL, LOUISIANA.

A distinctive feature of Roy Le Gaux's artistry is his "barn door art." A number of his carvings such as "Hanging Mallard" are in the style of the *trompe l'oeil* artists of the nineteenth century. His skills in taxidermy and as a commercial artist serve him well. From carving working decoys, he turned to decorative bird carving in 1973.

Le Gaux's talent as a "fool-the-eye" artist is such that a photograph of one of his paintings was almost included in this book as a carving.

Of the many honors accorded him for his wildfowl art, Roy Le Gaux is proudest of having been made an honorary senator by the state of Louisiana.

96

Bald Eagle, Richard Le Master.

Willet, Richard Le Master.

RICHARD LE MASTER, CHILLICOTHE, ILLINOIS.

Most of Dick Le Master's professional life has been spent making models—70,000 of them, ranging from atom structures to working models of steel mills. In 1970 he was asked to carve a decoy for a friend. He writes:

When I build a model, I have plans, or the real thing to study. I bought some mallards and tried to study them. It did not take me long to realize that there had to be a better way.

I built a plastic box, lined it with mylar and observed and photographed ducks without their knowing they were being watched. I later developed several other miniature studios and to date, I have taken approximately 17,000 pictures of ducks.

The Decade of the 1970's

In 1976 Le Master wrote and published *Wildlife in Wood*, its text and photographs a tremendous boon to carvers of waterfowl. The blue-winged teal hen emerging from wood on the jacket of that book was carved and painted in six and one-half hours, a feat he has never come near duplicating since. "It was one of those creations that was meant to be...it seems to be the one that people remember." "A Teal Hen with Young" was one of a group of carvings by various artists exhibited in the National Collection of Fine Arts at the Smithsonian Institution in 1980.

Dick has just brought out *The Le Master Method of Waterfowl Identification*, a new system for identifying ducks by their bills, absolutely distinctive between species, and between drake and hen within species.

Peregrine Falcon with Green-winged Teal, Gilbert Maggioni. Photo by Mike and Maggie Nichols.

Doves Flushing from Cornfield, Gilbert Maggioni.
Photo by Mike and Maggie Nichols.

GILBERT MAGGIONI, BEAUFORT, SOUTH CAROLINA.

"It is easy to imagine that a sorcerer has been at work casting a spell which, when broken, will release the wings to beat again and the flight pattern to continue." The sorcerers Maggie Nichols wrote of in *Field & Stream* were Gilbert Maggioni and Grainger McKoy. Their carvings of birds and habitat groups were assembled at the American Museum of Natural History in the spring of 1974.

Maggioni and McKoy, boon hunting companions and incidental carvers of decoys for themselves, happened to be in the fields near Chestertown, Maryland, in 1967 and decided to have a look at the birds being exhibited at the second biennial show sponsored by the Kent County chapter of the Maryland Ornithological Society.

Maggioni felt that the birds he saw were earth-bound, not airborne. Much of what takes place in a bird's life takes place in the air, not on the ground. Birds don't use the air just for travel, they *live* in the air. To express action-in-air, wing and tail feathers under stress — steering, holding position in response to the bird's "gyroscope" — Maggioni developed a technique of individual feather carving and insertion. When he showed up at the 1968 Ward Foundation's Wildfowl Carving and Art Exhibit with a wild turkey in flight, the art of decorative bird carving was revolutionized.

With comparatively few carvings in existence, Maggioni remains pre-eminent in the field. After he frees himself from his business involvements, Maggioni expects to return to his art.

The Decade of the 1970's

GRAINGER MCKOY, WADMALAW ISLAND, SOUTH CAROLINA.

Grainger McKoy, as a student at Clemson, accompanied Maggioni to the 1968 exhibit in Salisbury, Maryland, and witnessed the stir caused by Maggioni's treatment and dramatic posing of his wild turkey.

On the way home to South Carolina, Maggioni said to McKoy, "Get into this thing. I've seen what you can do. When you finish school, move to Beaufort. Just give it eighteen months and you will never regret it." After graduation in 1970, McKoy, with his wife, moved to Beaufort to study and work with Maggioni.

Deeply respecting each other's knowledge of birds as well as each other's mania for accuracy in color, confirmation, and proportion, the two artists worked together for the next year and a half. Maggioni's innovative techniques profoundly affected McKoy's development as a carver, yet the two men progressed in parallel, each reinforcing what was unique and individual in the other.

Before and since the exhibit of Maggioni's and McKoy's bird sculptures at the American Museum of Natural History in 1974, McKoy has devoted his full time to his art, lately completing a fifteen-bird composition, "Quail Covey Rise."

Green Wing Teal, Grainger McKoy.

Baby Chickadees, Ernest Muehlmatt. Photo courtesy of Wildlife World, Inc.

ERNEST F. MUEHLMATT, SPRINGFIELD, PENNSYLVANIA.

Art training combined with years as a floral designer in the family business gave Ernest Muehlmatt the background to enable him to switch careers in 1970. In the decade since, Muehlmatt has carved more than 5,000 birds and has won recognition across the country.

There was little demand for oriental flower arrangements in the florist trade, but Muehlmatt's skill and interest in this specialized design form helped him to invest the settings for his bird carvings with charm and originality. No matter how wide the variety of birds Muehlmatt produces, his baby chickadees are the perennial favorite.

JOHN N. MULLICAN, BOWIE, MARYLAND.

John Mullican's interest in nature began in his childhood days while fishing, hunting, and tramping in the woods of his native Maryland. His talent in art developed into a professional career as a painter of hunting dogs and wildlife.

Mullican fashioned his first bird carving in 1954, but it was at the first Wildfowl Carving and Art Exhibit of the Ward Foundation in 1968 that John was stimulated to turn his hand to bird sculpture in wood.

Songbirds serve as models for most of his work. His carving of the Maryland state bird and flower is on permanent exhibit at the State Capitol in Annapolis, an honor which especially pleases the native son.

Bufflehead, John Mullican. Photo by Tom Johnson.

Pileated Woodpeckers, John Mullican.
Photo by Tom Johnson.

JIM PALMER, CHARLESTON, SOUTH CAROLINA.

One of the rewards of bird carving for Jim Palmer is that it is a way of keeping in touch with his rural heritage. He spent his childhood on Wadmalaw Island off the coast of South Carolina, where he gained an appreciation for nature which has never dimmed.

His penchant for drawing and painting birds when he was in grade school was reinforced by a brief period of art instruction when he was twelve.

After army service and a stint as skipper-owner of a shrimp boat, Palmer moved to Charleston. While pursuing his livelihood in business, he longed to re-create in some way the natural environment he had left behind. Following his early bent, he took up carving; with his birds he reunites himself with nature and brings the viewer into that world as well.

Day's End, William Hanemann.

Robin, Jack and Bette Holt. Photo by Tom Johnson.

White-throated Sparrow, Gladys Hopkins. Photo by Richard Burke.

Pheasant Family, William J. Koelpin. Photo by Hans Keerl Studio.

Pintails, Gilbert Maggioni. Photo by Orlando Wootten, courtesy of the Ward Foundation.

Clapper Rails, Grainger McKoy. Photo by Arie DeZanger.

Oystercatcher, Grainger McKoy. Photo by Ted Borg.

Sparrow Hawk, Grainger McKoy. Photo by Ted Borg.

Marsh Wren, Grainger McKoy. Photo by Ted Borg.

Sora Rail, Grainger McKoy. Photo by Ted Borg.

Spotted Sandpiper, Grainger McKoy. Photo by Ted Borg.

Quail, Ernest Muehlmatt. Photo by Tom Johnson.

Clapper Rails with Snail, Anthony J. Rudisill. Photo by Steve Budman, Ward Foundation, courtesy of Wildlife World, Inc.

Goshawk with Crow (front), John Scheeler. Photo by Jack Lawler, III.

Goshawk with Crow (back), John Scheeler. Photo by Jack Lawler, III.

Gyrfalcon, John Scheeler. Photo courtesy the Ward Foundation. Wildlife World, Inc. 1980 First in Show, Decorative Lifesize — Professional Class.

Yellow-shafted Flickers, John Mullican. Photo by Tom Johnson.

Ruffed Grouse, John Scheeler. Photo courtesy the Ward Foundation.

Woodcock, Robert and Virginia Warfield.

Owl and Mouse, John Scheeler. Photo courtesy the Ward Foundation.

Pied-bill Grebe with Chick, Robert and Virginia Warfield. Photo by Tom Johnson.

Red-tailed Hawk, Phillip Zeller.

Laughing Gull, Ken Scheeler. Photo by Tom Johnson.

Canada Goose with Goslings, Hans Bolte.

Oldsquaw Drake, Larry Hayden. Photo by Les Ward, courtesy of Wildlife World, Inc.

Black Ducks, Grainger McKoy. Photo courtesy of the Ward Foundation.

Green-winged Teal, Robert Kerr.

Cinnamon Teal, Jim Sprankle. Photo by Tom Johnson.

Hen Canvasback, Larry Hayden. Photo by
Les Ward.

Pintail Drake, Tan Brunet.

Shoveler Drake, Jim Sprankle. Photo by Mike Hopiak.

Green Herons, Anthony J. Rudisill.

A.J. RUDISILL, WEST ATLANTIC CITY, NEW JERSEY.

"Tony" Rudisill first achieved success in wildlife art with his painstakingly researched, meticulously detailed paintings. He brings the trained artist's sense of composition to his sculptures and carries over none of the limitations of flat art to the three dimensional medium. Although there is a so-called "front" side to his carvings, it is rewarding to view them from any angle.

The exquisite poise of the clapper rails reaching for a snail and the delicate balance of the green herons contending for a crab attest to Rudisill's keenly observant eye and intimacy with nature.

JOHN SCHEELER, MAY'S LANDING, NEW JERSEY.

In "death" the crow is as close to nature as any of the "live" birds in the exhibition hall. John Scheeler's "Goshawk with Crow" is literally thrilling. The predator and victim are caught at a moment of awful truth.

Scheeler started bird carving in earnest about ten years ago after he attended a Ward Foundation Wildfowl Art Exhibit. He was astonished at what he saw, and "felt that this was for me." He knew a lot about wood and paint from his trade as a house painter, he had made some decoys, and he had had a few months of art lessons.

So he started carving, painting and posing hawks, owls and falcons and their prey. His method of conditioning the wood before he paints results in extraordinarily "soft" feathers and fur. His instinct for lifelike poses comes naturally, from his knowledge of wild creatures..

Scheeler returns to the Ward Foundation's World Championship Carving Competitions each year and has to date won five championships in the eleven-year history of the competition.

DEL SMITH, OTIS, OREGON.

Del Smith's first carving was a decoy. He says, "For the first few years I carved only decoys, did the contest bit, and won my share of ribbons."

Then Smith took a "side road" into decorative bird carving. His feeling for wood is akin to his feeling for birds, so he wanted "a piece that looks like a Wilson's snipe, for example; but like a *wood-carving* of a Wilson's snipe. So I started leaving tool marks. I like to see them in a wood-carving—just as I like to see brush strokes in an oil painting."

Smith has exhibited on both coasts in shows including the Waterfowl Festival in Easton, Maryland, and at the Palm Springs Desert Museum, Palm Springs, California.

Black Neck Stilt, Del Smith. Photo courtesy of Wildlife World, Inc.

Killdeer with Young, Ron Tepley. Photo courtesy of Wildlife World, Inc.

RON TEPLEY, RACINE, WISCONSIN.

Migratory waterfowl, game birds, and birds of prey are the chief subjects of Tepley's carvings. He has a particular interest in hawks.

Although he wins in both decoy and decorative categories in competition, Tepley likes the challenge inherent in ornamental-realistic carving. With his familiarity with birds in the wild, he is able to combine accuracy of form and plumage with artistic composition.

RICHARD AND VIRGINIA TROON, GRANT'S PASS, OREGON.

Dick and Jinx Troon began to sell their wildlife carvings in 1969. They have carved and painted nearly one hundred species of waterfowl, aquatic birds, and birds of prey, excluding songbirds. A distinctive feature of their treatment is that rather than using glass eyes, they carve and paint the eyes of their creatures.

The Troons' work is exhibited and well-known on both coasts.

ROBERT AND VIRGINIA WARFIELD, JAFFREY, NEW HAMPSHIRE.

The Warfield bird carvings are the yield of a joint effort, a fruitful partnership indeed. Their creations are the result of full collaboration at every stage.

Robert carves the basic shape — "a subtractive process," he calls it. He believes removing *enough* wood is critical to an accurate and artistic final rendering. After the larger feather groups are incised by Robert, Virginia burns in the spines and barbs of each individual feather. They hand each piece back and forth until they are satisfied that it is ready for Virginia to color with oil paints.

Ruffed Grouse, Robert and Virginia Warfield.

The Decade of the 1970's

Robert and Virginia Warfield have sculpted birds in every category, and have contrived settings of a degree of complexity ranging from small songbirds on simple bases to a wood duck drake with cattails and a painted turtle, as well as a sculpture depicting a pair of ring neck pheasants. A white cockatoo is the most exotic carving, the chickadee the most familiar. Only the creators can judge the challenge each subject presents. Virginia says that in some ways the cock pheasant with its fifty shades of color is less difficult to paint than a chickadee.

A favorite quotation of the Warfields comes from Jacob Bronowski's *Ascent of Man*: "The most powerful drive in the ascent of man is his pleasure in his own skill. He loves to do what he does well, and having done it well, he loves to do it better."

Red-tailed Hawk, Phillip Zeller. Photo by Gordon N. Converse.

Marsh Wren, Phillip Zeller. Photo by Phillip N. Converse.

PHILLIP E. ZELLER, EAST ARLINGTON, VERMONT.

Before moving to Vermont, Phillip Zeller lived for many seasons in Maine, near enough to Wendell Gilley to be inspired and encouraged by the veteran master.

As is often the case, much of Zeller's familiarity with the subjects of his carvings comes from his love for duck hunting, especially on the Cape Cod shores and marshes so well-known to Elmer Crowell.

Zeller is a very disciplined, very observant carver, determined to glean every bit of information pertinent to his subjects and his art. He is also extremely versatile. His range runs from hawks, ducks, and pheasants to bluebirds and hummingbirds. It is his ambition to portray every North American bird.

Zeller has exhibited for several years in the Leigh Yawkey Woodson Art Museum's annual Bird Art Exhibit. (His entry in 1979, a kingfisher, was selected for inclusion in the exhibit at the Smithsonian Institution in 1980.) Before sending his red-tailed hawk to Wausau, Wisconsin, for the 1980 show, Zeller took it outdoors to be photographed. At the appearance of the carved bird, small birds nearby disappeared, testament indeed to the realistic quality of Zeller's work.

5

The Waterfowl Specialists

In *The Atlantic Flyway* Robert Elman writes:

> Many paths lead to nature's exquisite labyrinth. Some may find it strange that my own perception of nature has been most powerful and moving when it occurred within the hunting context, but it is so; in my experience, the activity of hunting provides an access to nature second to none and far richer than most.

That statement is seconded by most of the carvers in this book from the "old choppers" to the newer "buzzers." Some remain ardent hunters; for others it has become impossible to shoot creatures not immediately necessary for economic or physical survival, the need for meat having been met by stockyard and supermarket.

Regardless, the psychic bonding between hunter and quarry, between artist and subject has taken place. This alliance has been most directly expressed in the making of decoys. As times have changed and the carver has sought to master greater challenges, the hunting stool has developed into a "contemporary wildfowl carving." There is, as one carver aptly put it, "a difference between a floating decoy and a carving of a duck swimming."

The following carvers have chiefly or entirely confined themselves to portraying waterfowl, the birds most associated with hunting. Their achievements cannot be overlooked in a survey of decorative bird carving.

HANS BOLTE, TROY, MICHIGAN.

Hans Bolte was born in West Germany, where at the age of fourteen he began his apprenticeship as a wood pattern maker. When he came to the United States in 1957 he continued in that occupation.

His customers and friends had confidence that he could do anything in wood he wanted to—or they wanted him to—and one encouraged him to make a goose from wood. In 1974 Bolte made his first decoy and entered it in a major competition where it took a blue ribbon.

He became known as the "goose man" for his many prize winners, but his decorative ducks brought home just as many awards. His canvasback sleeper was exhibited in the National Collection of Fine Arts exhibition in 1980.

The Canada goose is Hans Bolte's favorite bird, and spectators have an irresistible urge to reach out and touch the "soft feathers and down" of the "Mother Goose with Goslings."

TAN BRUNET, GALLIANO, LOUISIANA.

Tan Brunet, in the lobby of the Tidewater Inn in Easton, Maryland, said of the stunning pintail under his arm: "This bird's going to fly to Tennessee after the show." For a moment one had a picture of the sprig flapping its own wings to make the trip, so lifelike was the carving.

Brunet keeps no patterns, modeling his ducks after his pen-raised birds. Attacking the wood block with knife and hatchet, he produces ducks that fly to collectors' shelves as soon as the painted feathers dry.

Oystercatcher, Delbert Daisey. Photo by Dan Brown.

Pintail Hen, Delbert Daisey. Photo by Dan Brown.

DELBERT "CIGAR" DAISEY, CHINCOTEAGUE, VIRGINIA.

Dan Brown wrote the following at the Philadelphia Wildfowl Exposition, 1980:

Delbert "Cigar" Daisey. Decoy maker, fisherman, hunting guide, poacher, duck trapper, outlaw, all describe "Cigar" Daisey.

Over his fifty-three years he has spent his time making a living on, or near, the water, hunting and trapping in the winter, and fishing and clamming in the summer. Much of his reputation was gained in his earlier years, when like many in the area, he felt the ducks and geese were sent by Mother Nature and not the federal government. The trapping and selling of wild ducks was a way of life for many, and Delbert Daisey was king of the duck trappers.

Cigar's fierce competitiveness is the reason for his success whether he is trapping the wily fox or carving decoys. His first decoys were made in his early teens. His finest work wasn't to come until the middle and late sixties when he became a consistent winner in competitive shows, particularly with the black duck, considered by him to be the king of the ducks. In his lifetime he has dispatched over 30,000 ducks.

Now he hunts only occasionally and has learned a new appreciation for birds and has great concern for their protection and conservation. His activities are limited to observing and carving his fine reproductions of God's creatures.

Cigar's nickname was earned years ago late one evening when with friends he carried out an expedition onto a refuge to rob duck traps set for banding the birds. Delbert Daisey (being a heavy cigar smoker at the time) lost all of his cigars in the trap. The next day the authorities spent the day around Chincoteague looking for someone who smoked that brand. Til this day, Delbert Daisey is known as Cigar.

Drake Merganser, John B. Garton. Photo by Tom Johnson.

Widgeon, John B. Garton. Photo by Tom Johnson.

122

Mallard, John B. Garton. Photo by Tom Johnson.

JOHN B. GARTON, JASPER, ONTARIO, CANADA.

J.B. Garton was born in Manitoba, a principal pit stop on the Central Flyway. He started carving decoys in 1942, especially black ducks, although many successful competitions later it is the blue-winged teal that springs to mind when Garton is mentioned. A pair of blue-wings won in the first World Class Carving Championship, sponsored by the Ward Foundation in 1971.

Garton used to call himself "a decoy carver." He can do that no longer, for his highly decorative mergansers, widgeons — all species of ducks — now share display space with game birds — quail and ruffed grouse.

123

Oldsquaw Hen, Ken Gleason. Photo by Eldridge Arnold.

KEN GLEASON, DARIEN, CONNECTICUT.

By 1976 Ken Gleason had won more than one hundred blue ribbons for reproductions of his "old friends," the diving ducks. He made their acquaintance while lobstering as a teenager, when his constant offshore companions were mergansers, scoters and golden eyes.

Gleason's circle of friends has widened to include sportsmen who share his enthusiasm for the outdoor life. One of these newer companions supplied a photo of Ken Gleason's "Old-squaw Hen," modeled after one of Ken's "old friends."

LARRY HAYDEN, FARMINGTON HILLS, MICHIGAN.

Larry Hayden was a professional illustrator until 1979 when he decided to devote all his working hours to wildlife art. He began carving decoys for his own use in 1963, and when he entered contests in the 1970's, his decoys often had to compete among themselves in the final judging, all others having been eliminated.

The water of the judging tank is the only water Hayden's decorative carved birds float in, so coveted are they by collectors. The demand for his depictions of ducks is met in some measure by his "flat art," including prints of the first Nevada Duck Stamp in 1979, and the 1980 Michigan Duck Stamp.

Hayden thinks the popularity of "bird art" stems from the desire of many who want a "small piece of nature" in their homes as our natural resources dwindle.

124

The Waterfowl Specialists

DON MORLEY, HEUVELTON, NEW YORK.

Don Morley has taught himself everything he knows about carving. He did it with the help of his friends in his backyard—the many varieties of ducks and geese he raises.

He has developed his style on his own, a style which has won him a fair share of awards. Morley devotes full time to his carving now, abetted by his outdoor recreations, hunting and fishing.

JAY POLITE, NEW CASTLE, DELAWARE.

Jay Polite, born and raised in lower Delaware, is another carver whose knowledge of waterfowl has been learned as a duck hunter. That he has learned certain of nature's lessons thoroughly is exemplified by his ducks, which won many ribbons in the 1970's. He often abstains from competition now because he is judging; he often abstains from judging now because his pupils are competing for the top awards.

Polite's interest in carving decorative ducks lies in the artistic challenge they present.

Ruddy Duck Hen, Don Morley. Photo by Tom Johnson.

KEN SCHEELER, VINELAND, NEW JERSEY.

Ken Scheeler's best known carvings are his decorative waterfowl.

He also does waterbirds such as the laughing gull. That he has seen its live counterpart is a success story of the early conservationists. At the turn of the century the risible gull had been all but eliminated in its northern range of Nantucket and the marshes of Long Island and New Jersey.

Over the protests of the fashion industry and its customers (one woman objected that only the *wings* of gulls were used on hats), laws were passed to prevent the birds' extinction in the cause of fancy millinery.

On the subject of decorative-bird hats, George Miksch Sutton recalls in *Bird Student* that church services, when he was little, were

> hard to endure unless a hat on some woman in a pew in front of ours happened to have a bird (or part of a bird) on it. With pencil in hand and hymn-book in lap, I could draw to my heart's content... I recall especially a veritable whorl of terns, each footless and with spread wings, encircling the crown of a straw hat.

Hooded Merganser, Jim Sprankle. Photo by Tom Johnson.

Black Duck, Jim Sprankle. Photo by Tom Johnson.

JAMES D. SPRANKLE, KIRKWOOD, NEW YORK.

When he was still a boy, Jim Sprankle was proficient enough at taxidermy to prepare specimens for the Indiana Conservation Department. A paternal heritage of skilled woodworking and a passion for hunting prepared him, too, for his career as a top-flight carver of ducks.

An interim career as a major league baseball pitcher proved to Sprankle how intensely he wished to win. So, reckoning that competition would improve his carving abilities, Jim entered the major contests. The walls of his home are blue with his honors.

For continuing education and relaxation, Sprankle raises ducks in his backyard and pond. He also still hunts, but finds it increasingly difficult to shoot teal, for instance, after he has known their kind as pets. Mallards are different, though; he says they are bullies in the pen, and "they come easy after what they do to teal."

RANDY TULL, HAYWARD, WISCONSIN.

"I'm a waterfowl fanatic," Randy Tull says. When he was hospitalized after an accident nearly a decade ago he took up carving as therapy, and a year later he was able to turn his therapy into a career. Many awards later, his customers are collectors and sportsmen.

One wonders how many of these softly-feathered, bright-eyed carvings get taken down to the lakes and rivers. Surely not the "Pintail Drake in Nuptial Display" that was exhibited at the National Collection of Fine Arts show, sponsored by the Smithsonian Institution in 1980.

DAN WILLIAMS, REISTERTOWN, MARYLAND.

The first time Dan Williams visited Maryland, he decided that the state where so many ducks and geese winter was the place for him. He immediately pulled up stakes, moved to Maryland and began to carve and paint ducks without any previous instruction.

It was a labor of love which has become his full-time occupation. He credits much of his success and joy in his work to his friend and mentor, Don Briddell.

Gadwall Drake, Dan Williams.

The Waterfowl Specialists

JOSEF WOOSTER, ASHLEY, OHIO.

When he was six, Josef Wooster began taking lessons in art; when he was ten, he was whittler of replacement heads for the family rig of decoys, the originals having been shot off by the less skilled marksmen in the group.

Wooster studied art and waterfowl, and the two interests are met in the carvings he fashions with rasp and riffler of loons, coots, grebes, and every species of duck and goose native to North America.

Of that great variety, the wood duck is the bird most closely associated with Wooster. A Wooster drake woodie was included in the National Collection of Fine Arts Exhibition of Art Depicting Birds at the Smithsonian Institution in 1980.

Mallard Drake, Wendell Gilley. Photo by Dori Selene Rockefeller.

Several of the carvers mentioned in earlier chapters are as well-known for their carvings of waterfowl as for their carvings of other species, which were illustrated previously. A sampling of waterfowl carvings by these versatile carvers follows.

Black Duck, Arnold Melbye. Photo by Scorchy Tawes Photo.

Mona Mallard, Don Briddell.

Buffleheads, J. J. Iski. Photo courtesy of Wildlife World, Inc.

Flying Blue-winged Teal Hen, Dan Brown.

Red-breasted Merganser, A. Elmer Crowell.

Green-winged Teal, A. Elmer Crowell.

Black Duck Sleeper, "Shang" Wheeler.

Preening Pintail Drake, Lem Ward.

Preening Canada Goose, Lem Ward.

133

Red-breasted Merganser, Harold Haertel. Photo courtesy of Wildlife World, Inc.

Oldsquaw, Oliver Lawson. Photo by Jerry Fine.

Afterword

Art needs no justification. The masters of decorative bird carving can be credited with stimulating interest in and understanding of birds in the wild, but this does not mean they should be considered artists on this basis alone.

To record faithfully and to reproduce with great skill is not necessarily to create art. A certain level of competence in observation and technique is not enough; an artist must bring more to his work. He must invest it with his own creative thought, his personal reactions to what he sees and knows. Although this book deals with the carved and painted bird, exemplifying the union of natural science and artistic skill, it would be ignorant indeed to regard information conveyed as indispensable to art.

Charles "Chippy" Chase of Maine, an exhibitor in the first Chestertown show; John T. Sharp of Ohio, whose compositions enthrall at major shows; and Vaughn Burlingham of Sausalito, California, whose seabirds are exhibited in museums and galleries, express their knowledge and creativity with shaped, naturally finished sculptures. Though their carvings give no information about color nor details of plumage, they are hardly less aesthetic than realistic renderings.

Neither is incompleteness an absolute barrier to what may be termed art. In Dick Le Master's "Teal Hen with Young," the young emerge from wood as well as shell, and Grainger McKoy's "Snipe" takes flight from its wooden bondage. One has a sense that the creatures have been freed from the wood, that they have been waiting for the carver's life-revealing skills. They are incomplete, yet they have the power to move the viewer, an essential quality of art.

Virtuosity in execution and complexity of composition can be influential factors, but they are not the determining ones. Admiration is not necessarily appreciation, though it may be; excitation is not necessarily exaltation, yet it may be.

There is an attitude becoming more prevalent among carvers and the public that these birds sculptured in wood are more appropriately displayed in museums and galleries than in contests and craft shows. Competition, as it stimulates and educates, can be helpful in the development of a carver, but established standards also can have the effect of stifling creativity. Even though he is replicating inanimate or animate objects, an artist works to an inner vision,

Teal Hen with Young, Richard Le Master. Photo courtesy of Leigh Yawkey Woodson Art Museum.

not to written rules and regulations, though his final creation may be acceptable within those limits, also.

Art cannot be judged against itself. William Schultz points out that as it is "ludicrous to rank the work of Homer, Remington, or Russell as first, second, or third, so it is ludicrous to rank the work of America's top notch carvers."

Is it Art? Two criteria must be met, it seems to me: the creator must communicate what is intensely personal and unique to him, and the work must convey what cannot be expressed in words—the ineffable essence of his subject.

The judgment, to borrow from a rusty adage, lies in the mind and spirit of the observer, with the assessment of his highly subjective eye.

136

Emerging Snipe, Grainger McKoy.

Bibliography

ALLEN, ARTHUR A. *Stalking Birds with Color Camera*. Washington, D.C.: National Geographic Society, 1951.

BARBER, JOEL. *Wildfowl Decoys*. New York: Dover Publications, 1954.

BERKEY, BARRY, et al. *Pioneer Decoy Carvers*. Cambridge, Md.: Tidewater Publishers, 1977.

BLANCHAN, NELTJE. *Game Birds*. New York: Doubleday, Page & Co., 1904.

BURK, BRUCE. *Game Bird Carving*. New York: Winchester Press, 1972.

——. *Waterfowl Studies*. New York: Winchester Press, 1976.

CHAPMAN, FRANK M. *Bird Life*. New York: D. Appleton & Co., 1906.

——. *Handbook of Birds of Eastern North America*. New York: Dover Publications, Inc., 1966.

CHEEVER, BYRON. *L. T. Ward & Bro. Wildfowl Counterfeiters*. Heber City, Utah: North American DECOYS/ Hillcrest Publications, n.d.

COLIO, QUINTINA. *American Decoys*. Self-published, 1972.

EARNEST, ADELE. *The Art of the Decoy*. New York: Bramhall House, 1965.

EATON, ALLEN H. *Handicrafts of New England*. New York: Bonanza Books, 1949.

ELMAN, ROBERT. *The Atlantic Flyway*. Tulsa: Winchester Press, 1980.

——. *The Great American Shooting Prints*. New York: Ridge Press/Alfred A. Knopf, 1972.

Fifty-third Annual Report of the Commissioners of Fisheries and Game for the Year ending November 30, 1918. Boston: Commonwealth of Massachusetts, 1919.

FLECKENSTEIN, HENRY A., JR. *Decoys of the Mid-Atlantic Region*. Exton, Penn.: Schiffer Publishing Ltd., 1979.

——. *Shore Bird Decoys*. Exton, Penn.: Schiffer Publishing Ltd., 1980.

FORBUSH, EDWARD HOWE. *Birds of Massachusetts and Other New England States*. 3 vols. Massachusetts Department of Agriculture, 1925, 1927, 1929.

——. *Game Birds, Wildfowl and Shorebirds*. Massachusetts State Board of Agriculture, 1917.

GILLEY, WENDELL. *Bird Carving*. New York: Bonanza Books, 1961.

——. *The Art of Bird Carving*. Spanish Fork, Utah: Hillcrest Publications, Inc., 1972.

JOHNSGARD, PAUL A. *The Bird Decoy*. Lincoln: University of Nebraska Press, 1976.

KORTRIGHT, F.H. *The Ducks, Geese and Swans of North America*. Washington, D.C.: Wildlife Management Institute, and Harrisburg, Penn.: The Stackpole Co., 1967.

LE MASTER, RICHARD. *Wildlife in Wood*. Chicago: Contemporary Books, Inc., 1978.

MACKEY, WILLIAM F., JR. *American Bird Decoys*. New York: E.P. Dutton and Co., 1965.

MARCHAM, FREDERICK GEORGE, ed. *Louis Agassiz Fuertes & The Singular Beauty of Birds*. New York: Harper and Row, 1971.

MATTHIESSEN, PETER. *The Wind Birds*. New York: Viking Press, 1973.

McKINNEY, J. EVANS. *Decoys of the Susquehanna Flats and Their Makers*. Hockessin, Del.: The Holly Press, 1978.

MURPHY, CHARLES F. *Working Plans for Working Decoys*. New York: Winchester Press, 1979.

MURPHY, STANLEY. *Martha's Vineyard Decoys*. Boston: David R. Godine, 1978.

PARMALEE, PAUL W., and LOOMIS, FORREST P. *Decoys and Decoy Carvers of Illinois*. De Kalb: Northern Illinois University Press, 1969.

PEARSON, T. GILBERT, editor-in-chief. *Birds of America*. Garden City, New York: Garden City Books, 1936.

PETERSON, ROGER TORY. *A Field Guide to the Birds, Eastern Land and Water Birds*. Boston: Houghton Mifflin Co., 1963.

——. *A Field Guide to the Birds East of the Rockies*. Boston: Houghton Mifflin Co., 1980.

PORTER, ELIOT. *Birds of North America*. New York: E.P. Dutton & Co., 1972.

POUGH, RICHARD H. *Audubon Water Bird Guide*. Garden City, New York: Doubleday and Co., Inc., 1951.

RICHARDSON, R.H., ed. *Chesapeake Bay Decoys*. Crow Haven Publishers. 1973.

ROBBINS, CHANDLER S.; BRUNN, B.; ZIM, H.S.; AND SINGER, A. *A Guide to Field Identification. Birds of North America*. New York: Golden Press, 1966.

SMITH, ELMER L. *American Wildfowl Decoys from Folk Art to Factory*. Lebanon, Penn.: Applied Arts Publishers, 1974.

SORENSON, HAROLD D. *Decoy Collector's Guide*. Volumes 1, 2, 3, and 6. Burlington, Iowa: Harold D. Sorenson, 1963, 1964, 1965, and 1977.

STARR, GEORGE ROSS, JR. *Decoys of the Atlantic Flyway*. New York: Winchester Press, 1974.

——. *How to Make Working Decoys*. New York: Winchester Press, 1978.

STEFFERUD, ALFRED, ed. *Birds In Our Lives*. The United States Department of the Interior, 1965.

STOUT, GARDNER D., ed.; MATTHIESSEN, PETER, text; CLEM, ROBERT VERITY, paintings; and PALMER, RALPH S. *The Shorebirds of North America*. New York: Viking Press, 1967.

SUTTON, GEORGE MIKSCH. "A Pet Road Runner." In *Bird Lore*, Frank M. Chapman, ed. Volume 15. Harrisburg, Penn. and New York: D. Appleton, 1913.

——. "Suggestive Methods of Bird Study: Pet Road Runners." In *Bird Lore*, Frank M. Chapman, ed. Vol. 17. Harrisburg, Penn. and New York: D. Appleton, 1915.

——. *Bird Student*. Austin: University of Texas Press, 1980.

——. *Fifty Common Birds of Oklahoma*. Norman: University of Oklahoma Press, 1961.

——. *To a Young Bird Artist*. Norman: University of Oklahoma Press, 1979.

TAWES, WILLIAM I. *Creative Bird Carving*. Cambridge, Md.: Tidewater Publishers, 1969.

WEBSTER, DAVID S., and KEHOE, WILLIAM. *Decoys at Shelburne Museum*. Shelburne, Vt.: The Shelburne Museum, 1961, 1971.

WETMORE, ALEXANDER, et al. *Song and Garden Birds of North America*. Washington, D.C.: National Geographic Society, 1965.

——. *Water, Prey, and Game Birds*. Washington, D.C.: National Geographic Society, 1964.

Bibliography

Catalogs, Programs and Exhibition materials produced by the following:

Birmingham Museum of Art, Birmingham, Alabama
Richard A. Bourne Co., Inc., Hyannis, Massachusetts
Cape Cod Museum of Natural History, Brewster, Massachusetts
Connecticut Audubon Society, Fairfield, Connecticut
R. C. Eldred Co., Inc., East Dennis, Massachusetts
National Audubon Society Exhibition at Kodak Gallery, New York, 1978
The Ward Foundation, Salisbury, Maryland
*The Waterfowl Festival, Easton, Maryland
The Leigh Yawkey Woodson Art Museum, Wausau, Wisconsin

* *Waterfowl Festival* is a registered trademark.

Index

Boldface page numbers indicate photographs of carvings.

143

Index

Produced under the direction of Joy Flora, Winchester Press
Book design and calligraphy by Quentin Fiore
Jacket design by Don E. Bryant
Text set in 11-point Baskerville by Columbia Publishing Company
Printed on 60-pound Warren's Olde Style by Christian Board of Publication
Bound in Holliston Mills cloth by The Becktold Company

E.L.F. 5/81
Oldsquaw

LYNN FOREHAND

ARNOLD MELBYE